Participant Workbook - Standing For Marriage Restoration

Jason Carver

STANDING SUPERNATURALLY MINISTRIES

© 2025 Jason Carver

Participant Workbook – Standing For Marriage Restoration
All rights reserved.

No part of this publication may be reproduced, stored in a retrieval system, or transmitted in any form or by any means—electronic, mechanical, photocopy, recording, or otherwise—without the prior written permission of the publisher, except for brief quotations used in reviews or teaching contexts.

Published by **Standing Supernaturally**
www.StandingSupernaturally.com
First Printing, August 2025

ISBN: 979-8-9912499-1-1

Scripture Acknowledgements

Scripture quotations are from the *ESV® Bible (The Holy Bible, English Standard Version®)*, copyright © 2001 by Crossway, a publishing ministry of Good News Publishers. Used by permission. All rights reserved.
www.crossway.org

Scripture quotations marked **NIV** are from the *Holy Bible, New International Version®, NIV®*. Copyright © 1973, 1978, 1984, 2011 by Biblica, Inc.™ Used by permission of Zondervan. All rights reserved worldwide.
www.Zondervan.com

Scripture quotations marked **TPT** are from *The Passion Translation®*. Copyright © 2017, 2018, 2020 by BroadStreet Publishing® Group, LLC. Used by permission. All rights reserved.
www.thepassiontranslation.com

Scripture quotations marked **NKJV** are from the *New King James Version®*. Copyright © 1982 by Thomas Nelson. Used by permission. All rights reserved.

Scripture quotations marked **NASB** are from the *New American Standard Bible®*, Copyright © 1960, 1962, 1963, 1968, 1971, 1972, 1973, 1975, 1977, 1995, 2020 by The Lockman Foundation. Used by permission. All rights reserved.
www.lockman.org

Scripture quotations marked **NLT** are from the *Holy Bible, New Living Translation*, copyright © 1996, 2004, 2015 by Tyndale House Foundation. Used by permission of Tyndale House Publishers, Inc., Carol Stream, Illinois 60188. All rights reserved.

Scripture quotations marked **KJV** are from the *King James Version*. Public domain.

Scripture quotations marked **AMP** are from the *Amplified® Bible*, Copyright © 1954, 1958, 1962, 1964, 1965, 1987 by The Lockman Foundation. Used by permission.

Scripture quotations marked **MSG** are from *THE MESSAGE*. Copyright © by Eugene H. Peterson, 1993, 1994, 1995, 1996, 2000, 2001, 2002. Used by permission of NavPress. All rights reserved.

Additional Content Acknowledgements

Portions of this workbook reference or are adapted from the following works:

Shaunti Feldhahn, *The Good News About Marriage: Debunking Discouraging Myths about Marriage and Divorce*, Multnomah Books, 2014. Used with gratitude and acknowledgment.

Jason Carver, *40 Day Stand For Marriage Restoration*, Standing Supernaturally Publishing, © 2024. Used by permission of the author.

Contents

About the Author	VI
Welcome To Standing For Restoration	1
How To Best Use This Curriculum	4
Honoring Our Stand and Spouse – Standing Class Contract	9
Session 1 – Foundations of Standing Supernaturally for Your Marriage	11
1. Session 1 – Day 1	17
2. Session 1 – Day 2	19
3. Session 1 – Day 3	21
4. Session 1 – Day 4	23
5. Session 1 – Day 5	25
6. Session 1 – Day 6	27
Session 2 – Spiritual Warfare Over Marriages	29
7. Session 2 – Day 1	35
8. Session 2 – Day 2	37
9. Session 2 – Day 3	39
10. Session 2 – Day 4	41
11. Session 2 – Day 5	43
12. Session 2 – Day 6	45
Session 3 – Reconciliation and Repentance	47
13. Session 3 – Day 1	55
14. Session 3 – Day 2	57

15.	Session 3 - Day 3	60
16.	Session 3 - Day 4	61
17.	Session 3 - Day 5	63
18.	Session 3 - Day 6	65

Session 4 - Standing With A Healed Heart: Grief, Shame, Fear, and Forgiveness — 67

Godly Grieving Over Your Marriage Activation Handouts — 75

19.	Session 4 - Day 1	79
20.	Session 4 - Day 2	81
21.	Session 4 - Day 3	83
22.	Session 4 - Day 4	85
23.	Session 4 - Day 5	87
24.	Session 4 - Day 6	89

Session 5 - The Promise, Price, and Power of Hope — 91

25.	Session 5 - Day 1	97
26.	Session 5 - Day 2	99
27.	Session 5 - Day 3	101
28.	Session 5 - Day 4	103
29.	Session 5 - Day 5	105
30.	Session 5 - Day 6	107

Session 6 - Standing Aware of the Enemy's Plans — 109

31.	Session 6 - Day 1	115
32.	Session 6 - Day 2	117
33.	Session 6 - Day 3	119
34.	Session 6 - Day 4	121
35.	Session 6 - Day 5	123
36.	Session 6 - Day 6	125

Session 7 - Standing With The Divine Perspective — 127

37.	Session 7 - Day 1	135
38.	Session 7 - Day 2	137

39. Session 7 – Day 3	139
40. Session 7 – Day 4	141
41. Session 7 – Day 5	143
42. Session 7 – Day 6	145
Session 8 – Standing In Victory!	147
43. Session 8 – Day 1	155
44. Session 8 – Day 2	157
45. Session 8 – Day 3	159
46. Session 8 – Day 4	161
47. Session 8 – Day 5	163
48. Session 8 – Day 6	165
Session 9 – A Spouse's Perspective	167
Conclusion: What's Next?	173
Appendix: Standing at a Distance When Necessary	175
Appendix: Video Guide – Answers	178
Appendix: Scripture List	184

ABOUT THE AUTHOR

Jason Carver is the founder of Standing Supernaturally for Marriage Restoration; he's a pastor, prophetic trainer, former tennis teaching professional and an international speaker. He currently travels the world teaching and preaching the message of hope that your marriage might look dead, but by the power of God it can be resurrected and better than ever. Jason believes that no matter what has happened in the past, your family can still walk in its Divine destiny.

His personal story of marital restoration is a prophetic picture of what God wants to do in anyone's life who is faithful and obedient to the promises of God. He coaches and teaches courses about how to supernaturally stand for family restoration. Jason loves seeing people experience the fullness that is available in scripture as they tap into the love, grace and power of God in their lives.

He also walks powerfully in prophetic ministry and travels internationally, teaching others how to grow in the prophetic gift and clearly hear the voice of God over their life. Jason is the founder of the Central Texas School of Supernatural Ministry, where he taught and trained people how to walk in and release the power of God in everyday situations.

Jason lives in Waco, Texas, with his beautiful wife, Christine, and his two wonderful daughters, Abby and Sydney. He teaches tennis at Baylor University during the school year and is the executive producer of the International TV ministry program "Ramiro Peña Ministries."

Jason carries supernatural hope and faith with joy and is passionate about seeing people walk in God's divine destiny for their lives. His personal goal is to carry hope in everything he does, and he believes joy and happiness are available to you no matter what you're experiencing.

STANDING SUPERNATURALLY MINISTRY RESOURCES

1. **Monthly Membership Program** — Our one-of-a-kind monthly membership program gives you special resources for standing for your marriage that you will see nowhere else. Sign up for a FREE 30-day trial today. www.StandingSupernaturally.com/Membership

2. **Standing Assessment Quiz** — Take our FREE 20-question quiz to see how well you are currently standing for your marriage. www.StandingSupernaturally.com/Assessment

3. **1-on-1 coaching/counseling session with Jason** — Talk one-on-one with Jason and have him speak directly about your stand and situation. For info on how to schedule a session with Jason, head to www.StandingSupernaturally.com/Counseling

4. **The Standing Supernaturally Academy** — This is our groundbreaking 12-week eCourse made specifically for those wanting to stand supernaturally for their marriage. www.Standing-Supernaturally.com/Academy

5. **Training Hub Media Site** — "Netflix style" website full of FREE sermons and resources regarding how to stand for your marriage. Training.StandingSupernaturally.com

6. **All Social Media Platforms** — @StandingSupernaturally, Standing Supernaturally for Marriage Restoration

7. **Ministry Website** — Find all details about everything we do and more resources on our website at www.StandingSupernaturally.com

FREE GIFT!
40 Prayers and Declarations to Pray Over Your Spouse
www.StandingSupernaturally.com/Gift

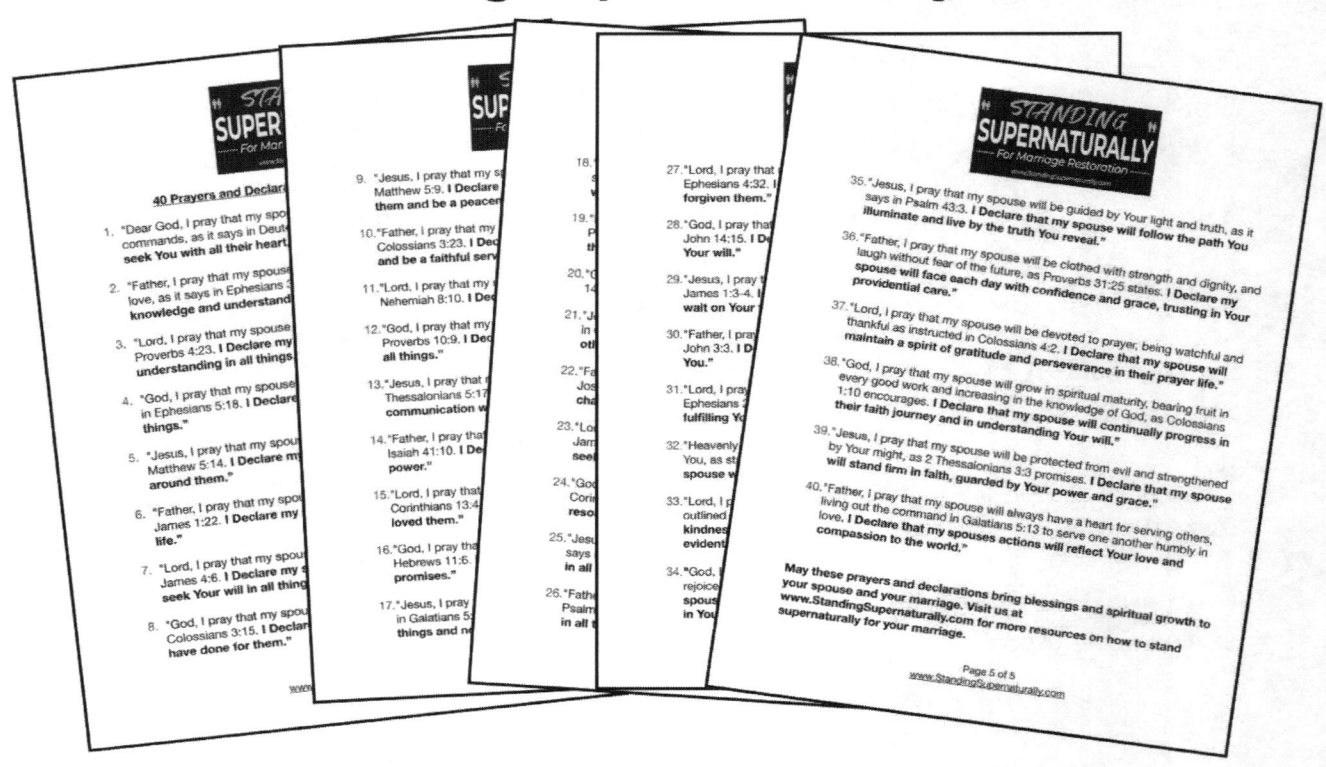

Thank you so much for purchasing this book! As a token of our appreciation and to further support you on your journey, we are excited to offer you a special gift: **"40 Prayers and Declarations to Pray Over Your Spouse."** This collection of biblically-based prayers and declarations is designed to enrich your prayer life and empower your stand for the restoration of your marriage. To receive your free gift, please visit ***www.StandingSupernaturally.com/Gift.***

We believe these prayers and declarations will be a powerful tool in your stand for marriage restoration!

Check out these other standing resources:

Jason's Best-Selling book: **"40 Day Stand For Marriage Restoration"**

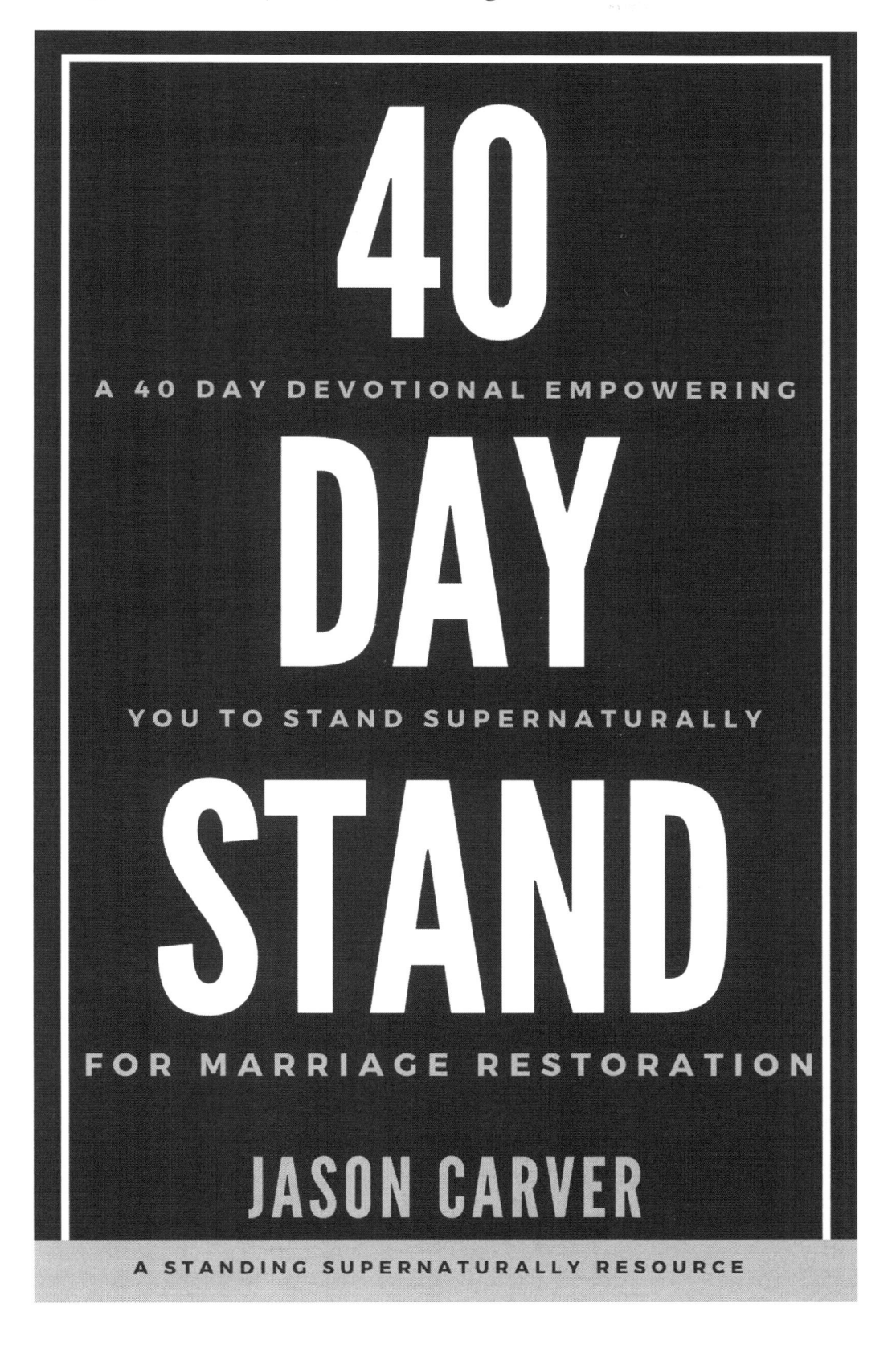

Check out these other 40 DAY STAND resources designed to go perfectly with this book…

40 DAY STAND Ecourse

Included in Ecourse

40 Daily Videos
Daily Emails From Jason Guiding You Through the Book
Weekly Prayer Challenges
Special Guest Interviews
Bonus content not in the book
PDF Download of Book

Register today at…
www.StandingSupernaturally.com/40DayStand

Coloring Your Stand For Marriage Restoration
Companion Coloring Book

Enhance your stand for marriage restoration in a fun and creative way with the "Coloring Your Stand For Marriage Restoration" companion coloring book. Designed to align perfectly with the 40 Day Stand daily devotionals. Dive even deeper into each of the daily themes and verses as you express your stand through the art of coloring. This coloring book adds a peaceful and reflective layer to your stand for marriage restoration. Immerse yourself in a world of creativity and art, making your daily stand bloom with colors!

Take advantage of these amazing tools to assist your stand for your marriage…

Take the Standing Assessment Quiz

How well are you "STANDING" for your marriage restoration?

SHORT 20 QUESTION ASSESSMENT — FREE!

From wondering if your marriage can be restored, to standing perfectly with God's power for restoration - learn what STAGE of standing supernaturally for marriage restoration you are at.

TAKE THE STANDING SUPERNATURALLY ASSESSMENT

GROW IN YOUR STAND FOR RESTORATION!

www.StandingSupernaturally.com/Assessment

Join the Monthly Membership Program - FREE TRIAL

SIGN UP NOW — FREE TRIAL

STANDING SUPERNATURALLY MONTHLY MEMBERSHIP PROGRAM

Come Stand Supernaturally TOGETHER with Jason & other supernatural standers

MEMBERSHIP BENEFITS
Monthly Membership Program Just For Standers!

JOIN NOW! FREE TRIAL

after 30 day trial it's only $25 a month (cancel anytime)

- ✓ Special Monthly Teaching from Jason
- ✓ Custom Declarations & Prayers made specifically for your spouse
- ✓ Monthly Live Q & A with Jason
- ✓ "After the Sermon" Sunday Night Zooms
- ✓ Private Members Only Facebook Group
- ✓ Standing Supernaturally Downloadable Wellness Check PDF
- ✓ Discounted Coaching Sessions with Jason
- ✓ Regional meetups with Jason (Qtrly)

www.StandingSupernaturally.com/Membership

Jason's book "Rekindling Love for Your Spouse as You Stand for Restoration"

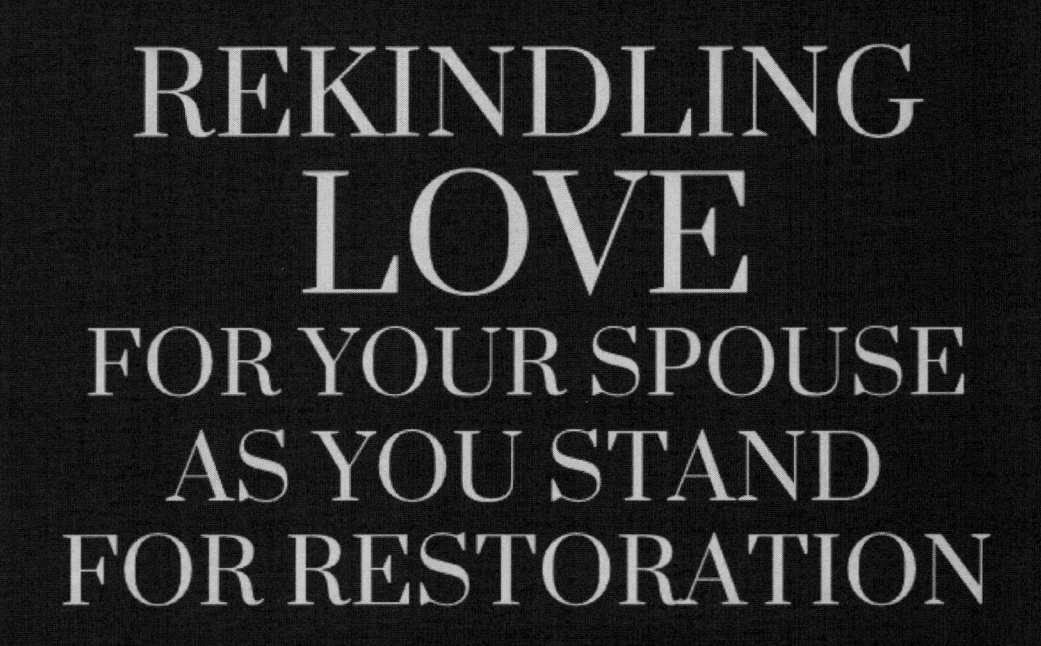

Welcome To Standing For Restoration

Welcome to the *Standing for Marriage Restoration* Small Group Video Curriculum, a 9-week, Holy Spirit-led journey designed to strengthen you as you stand supernaturally for the restoration of your marriage. Over these next 40 days, you are not just going through a workbook. You are stepping into a powerful move of God. This journey is rooted in the Word, filled with testimonies, and fueled by faith. It is an honor to walk with you during this sacred time. These pages will help equip and empower you as you trust God to restore what others said was finished.

This workbook will guide you through weekly small group sessions, five daily devotional exercises and daily reading from the book "40-Day Stand for Marriage Restoration." But this is not busywork. This is heart work. It is not about adding pressure to your schedule. It is about entering God's presence daily and letting Him strengthen you. Standing for your marriage is not a burden. It is a privilege and a supernatural invitation.

Each day, you will engage honestly with the questions, letting the Holy Spirit speak and lead. As you stay yielded and dependent on Him, you are going to be changed from the inside out. You will go from glory to glory, becoming stronger, more rooted, and more aligned with Heaven's heart for your marriage.

You will also do focused Bible reading and go through selected daily readings from "40-Day Stand for Marriage Restoration." This workbook will not follow the book chronologically. Instead, it guides you through it in an order that aligns with each week's teaching and theme.

Additional Resources Needed

Please make sure you have a copy of "40 Day Stand for Marriage Restoration," as this workbook is a companion, not a replacement. You can purchase it at www.StandingCurriculum.com or on Amazon.

Also available is the "Coloring Your Stand" coloring book. It is a peaceful way to engage with the daily theme and spend intentional time meditating on Scripture. You can also find this companion book in our store or on Amazon.

The Heart of the Journey

Marriage is a covenant, and the battle you are facing is not just natural. It is spiritual. That is why we go to God's Word. We are not just waiting for something to happen. We are actively standing in faith and allowing God to move. This journey is about becoming someone who is fully anchored in God, no matter what the circumstances look like.

The Power of God to Restore

Throughout Scripture, we see God raise what was dead, heal what was broken, and restore what seemed lost forever. In Ezekiel 37, He breathed life into a valley of dry bones. That is the kind of God we serve. The One who still restores, even now. And no matter how hopeless your marriage may feel, God can breathe life into it again.

My Personal Story

I have been where you are. My marriage was legally over. The papers were signed and the State of Texas said my marriage was officially dead. But God. He spoke. He led. He moved. And by His grace, He restored. It was not because of my strength. It was because of His. If He did it for me, He can do it for you.

If you have not seen our animated testimony, I encourage you to watch it. You can find it on www.StandingSupernaturally.com or on our YouTube channel, *Standing Supernaturally for Marriage Restoration*.

Some Encouragement as You Begin

- **Believe in God's Promises** – Scripture is full of promises for restoration. He has not forgotten you. Jeremiah 29:11 reminds us, "For I know the plans I have for you... plans to give you hope and a future."

- **Persist in Prayer** – Prayer is your weapon. Stay in conversation with God. James 5:16 says, "The prayer of a righteous person is powerful and effective."

- **Hold Onto Hope** – Do not let your circumstances steal your confidence. Jesus said, "With man this is impossible, but with God all things are possible" (Matthew 19:26).

- **Act in Faith** – Faith does not sit still. It moves. Let your actions reflect your belief that God is working even when you cannot see it.

- **Lean Into Community** – You were not meant to stand alone. Find strength in others standing with you. Hebrews 10:24 urges us to "spur one another on toward love and good deeds."

- **Trust in God's Timing** – Restoration does not always come quickly, but God's timing is always perfect. He is doing more behind the scenes than you can imagine. Do not rush the process. Trust the One who holds time in His hands.

Witnessing Miracles – The Power of Testimony

Your journey is going to impact others. Expect God to move. At the end of each day in "40 Day Stand for Marriage Restoration," you will read a real testimony of a restored marriage. Proof that God is still doing the impossible. Let those stories stir your faith.

What to Expect

This curriculum is designed to work hand in hand with the "40 Day Stand for Marriage Restoration" book and your small group journey.

Each week, you will:

- Watch a teaching video
- Participate in a group discussion
- Reflect daily in your workbook

Each day includes:

- **Daily Reading and Reflection** – Guided pages from the book and personal response
- **Scripture Focus** – Meditate and declare God's Word
- **Prayers and Declarations** – Align your words with God's truth
- **Activation Questions** – Take daily steps of obedience
- **Testimonies** – Be strengthened by what God has done in others

Commitment to the Journey

Friend, God is a Restorer. He loves turning hopeless situations into testimonies of His power. As you commit to this 40-day journey, know that you are not alone. God is walking with you every step. What He begins, He is faithful to complete.

Stay faithful. Be encouraged. Believe big. And know that with God, all things are possible.

You are not just reading a curriculum. You are stepping into a move of God. He is writing a testimony through your life that will encourage others to stand too.

Let this study ignite something in you that refuses to back down, that refuses to settle, and that dares to believe for restoration of your marriage, no matter what!

How To Best Use This Curriculum

This curriculum is designed to empower believers to stand firmly on God's promises for marriage restoration. Drawing from biblical principles and personal testimonies, participants will be guided to believe in God's ability to heal even the most broken and seemingly dead marriages. The journey through this curriculum is not just about gaining knowledge; it is about experiencing transformation, moving from hope to faith to witnessing God's restorative power in their lives.

Curriculum Overview:

There are several different approaches to engaging with this study. Below are the standard methods recommended to effectively facilitate this curriculum. Leaders are encouraged to seek the Holy Spirit's guidance, be creative, and prepare for significant breakthroughs in the participants' marriages and spiritual lives.

<u>A Special Message for Pastors:</u>

As a fellow pastor and ministry leader, we want you to know how deeply we honor the calling you carry and the work you do within your local church.

As a ministry, we are fully committed to and believe strongly in the power and purpose of the local church, and we know it is your deep desire to see your members walk in spiritual wholeness, experience healthy, restored marriages, and grow into mature disciples of Jesus. That's why we created *Standing for Marriage Restoration,* not just as a restoration curriculum but hopefully as a tool for transformation, revival, and healing within your congregation.

We understand the responsibility you carry as a shepherd, and we prepared a special video message just for pastors and church leaders to share the heart, theology, and vision behind *Standing for Marriage Restoration*. Whether you're exploring how to implement this curriculum in a small group, midweek class, Sunday school, or full churchwide campaign, this video will give you the clarity and confidence to move forward.

This "Message to Pastors" video, along with additional church leadership resources, is available at **www.StandingCurriculum.com.**

HOW TO USE THIS CURRICULUM:

1. CITY-WIDE SMALL GROUP STUDY

We believe one of the best ways to offer this course is to open it up to your entire city. There is a high probability that your own local church might not have a significant number of men and women standing for their marriages. Opening this class up for your entire community is a great way to help see your community come together and see the spirit of restoration take root in your area! It is common for churches to offer a diverse array of small group opportunities each season, featuring books, curriculum resources, and Bible studies. It's our prayer that "Standing for Marriage Restoration" becomes prominently included among these offerings, not only to serve your existing church community but also as an outreach to the entire city and surrounding areas.

This curriculum is particularly relevant as there are likely many individuals in your community who desire God to repair their marriages amidst separation or divorce, and may not be aware that there is a faith-based support system that believes in the healing and restoration of even "dead" marriages. Opening up these small groups to the broader community can provide crucial support and hope to those who might otherwise feel isolated in their struggles.

Community Engagement:

It is recommended that each small group consists of at least four to five people, with a recommended maximum of twelve – fifteen to maintain an intimate setting conducive to personal sharing and spiritual growth. Should the group exceed twelve members, consider splitting the group to preserve the setting's effectiveness or transitioning into a larger church class format. This flexibility will ensure that every participant receives ample attention and support.

Extending the Invitation:

To reach beyond the church walls, leaders are encouraged to promote these small groups throughout the city using various communication channels like social media, community bulletin boards, and local media outlets. This not only raises awareness about the availability of such a supportive resource but also highlights the church's role in fostering community and offering hope.

2. CHURCH CLASS / MIDWEEK CLASS / SUNDAY SCHOOL

Churches of all sizes offer discipleship classes designed to equip members and deepen spiritual growth. *Standing for Marriage Restoration* is a unique and powerful addition to your church's educational offerings. While it speaks directly to the pain and hope of marital healing, it also leads participants into deeper personal transformation, spiritual renewal, and restored intimacy with God.

Unlike traditional studies focused on finances, marriage roles, or general Bible studies, this curriculum centers on the spiritual discipline of standing in faith believing for the restoration of what looks broken beyond repair. It invites participants into a journey of surrender, intercession, and trust in God's supernatural ability to redeem.

Each class session is interactive and faith-building with:

- Weekly video teachings
- Guided discussion questions
- Scripture-based reflection
- Opportunities for group prayer and testimony
- A comprehensive Leader's Guide with answer keys and facilitation tips

This format is ideal for:

- Sunday School classes
- Midweek discipleship groups
- Marriage ministry gatherings
- Divorce recovery or separation support groups

We have heard from some churches that have even chosen to make this course a prerequisite before enrolling individuals in Divorce Care. By doing so, they give participants a chance to hear God's heart for restoration and respond in faith before pursuing permanent separation. This approach honors the marriage covenant while gently guiding people through their pain with biblical hope.

3. CHURCH-WIDE RESTORATION CAMPAIGN

"40 Days of Standing for Restoration"

For pastors desiring a church-wide move of healing and renewed faith, this curriculum can also be implemented as a full **church-wide campaign.** *40 Days of Standing for Restoration* is a Spirit-led initiative that unifies the entire congregation around the message of covenant restoration and God's power to redeem.

In this format:

- **Weekend sermons** align with each week's theme
- **Small groups, Sunday school, and life classes** follow the companion curriculum
- **Daily readings and declarations** from the "40 Day Stand for Marriage Restoration" book deepen personal application
- **Prayer focus and testimonies** build community and spiritual expectancy

This type of campaign not only ministers to those currently facing marriage challenges but also strengthens every member's faith in God's ability to restore what seems impossible. It builds a culture of covenant, intercession, and bold hope.

Churches that implement this model often see:

- Greater unity and compassion within the congregation
- Testimonies of breakthrough and healing
- A renewed hunger for God's presence and power
- Lasting discipleship fruit beyond the 40-day journey

4. INDIVIDUAL STUDY

While this curriculum is primarily designed for group settings, it can also be a powerful tool for personal study. Whether you are standing alone or simply desire a deeper understanding of what it means to stand for marriage restoration, this resource will help you engage with each topic, grow in faith, and apply God's truth to your life and marriage.

Please note: If you plan to go through this study individually, you will need the full Curriculum Kit, which includes:

- A USB containing the 9 Weekly Video Teachings
- The Leader's Guide
- The Participant Workbook
- The book "40 Day Stand for Marriage Restoration"
- The companion coloring book "Coloring Your Stand"

You can get the complete kit at **www.StandingCurriculum.com.**

That said, going through this study as part of a group is highly encouraged. Group settings foster community, accountability, and shared experiences, making the journey toward restoration even more impactful. If you do not have a group, please consider #5 below.

5. ONLINE SMALL GROUP STUDY

If you don't have a local church or small group currently offering *Standing for Marriage Restoration*, our ministry offers an online small group experience designed just for you.

These 9-week virtual gatherings are led by trained facilitators who are familiar with the curriculum and passionate about helping others stand for their marriages. Whether you're in a different city, country, or simply unable to find a group nearby, you don't have to go through this journey alone.

Participants in our online group's experience:

- The same weekly video teachings
- Live group discussions
- Powerful prayer support
- Encouragement from others who are also standing

This is the perfect option for those seeking a standing community, a faith-filled connection, and spiritual accountability in an online setting.

To join an online group, visit www.StandingCurriculum.com to find the next available session.

Honoring Our Stand and Spouse - Standing Class Contract

Commitment to Privacy, Respect, and Honor in Our Group

Welcome to the *Standing for Marriage Restoration* group. We are honored to walk this journey with you as we stand together in faith for the restoration of our marriages. To create a safe and respectful environment for everyone, we ask all participants to adhere to the following guidelines:

- **Confidentiality:** What is shared in this group stays in this group. This includes all discussions, personal stories, and prayer requests. I will not discuss the content of our group meetings with anyone outside of the group.

- **Anonymity:** I will not mention the names of participants' spouses or share the names of those who are in this class with others. I will respect each person's privacy and not disclose their participation in this group without their explicit permission.

- **Respect for Openness:** Understand that some participants may be more open than others about their marriage situations. I will honor everyone's choice in how they communicate their stand and respect the level of detail they choose to share.

- **Non-Judgmental Support:** While this class holds to the biblical worldview of marriage between a man and a woman, I also understand that there are different biblical views and interpretations on second marriages. I will not step into a judgmental role regarding whether or not a person should be standing for their marriage. If I disagree with their stand, I will keep it to myself and trust God will guide them correctly. I understand that arguments or debates on the validity of second and third marriages will not be entertained or tolerated during this group.

- **Unsolicited Advice:** I will refrain from giving unsolicited advice during group discussions.

- **Prayer Commitment:** The names of fellow participants listed below are for the purpose of daily prayer only. I will not share this list with anyone outside the group. This commitment ensures that I am supporting my fellow participants in prayer while maintaining confidentiality.

- **Fostering Hope:** I will refrain from sharing all the negative details I am currently encountering. I realize this has the potential to only bring discouragement to the entire group. I will choose to create a place of hope in our discussions, even though I am encountering great pain during this season. I understand that everyone here is also going through great difficulty and we are all in this together and will see healing in our marriages.

- **Speaking Honor and Blessings:** During this course, I will choose to speak honor and blessings over my spouse and others' spouses. I will choose to see my spouse and others' spouses as the Lord sees them, not defining them by their current actions and words. I declare that our spouses are made in God's image and have a divine destiny that will be fulfilled.

Write group member's and their spouse's names below for daily prayer:

1. _____
2. _____
3. _____
4. _____
5. _____
6. _____
7. _____
8. _____
9. _____
10. _____
11. _____
12. _____
13. _____
14. _____

"I declare that these families are GETTING RESTORED in Jesus' name!"

Signature: _____

Date: _____

Thank you for your commitment to creating a safe, supportive, and honoring environment for all participants. Together, we are trusting in God's power to restore each marriage.

Session 1 - Foundations of Standing Supernaturally for Your Marriage

In this opening session, "Foundations of Standing Supernaturally for Your Marriage," Pastor Jason Carver lays the groundwork for understanding what it means to stand in faith for your marriage restoration. He explains that standing supernaturally is not about ignoring the current reality of your situation but about trusting in God's power to bring healing and restoration to even the most broken circumstances. Through personal testimony and biblical truths, this session challenges you to build a firm foundation of faith, focus on God's promises, and reject the lies of hopelessness. You will be encouraged to see your stand as a spiritual partnership with God and to anchor yourself in His unshakable ability to resurrect what seems impossible.

"Standing for your marriage means trusting in God's power to heal all the current brokenness, even when it seems impossible. With God, nothing is too hard, and He is actively blessing, protecting, and resurrecting marriages. Even if others say it's over, remember that God is in the business of restoration. With unwavering faith and the supernatural power of God, your marriage can be resurrected and restored." – Jason Carver

To begin this first session, go around the group and read and fill out the "Honoring Our Stand and Spouse – Standing Class Contract."

Spend a few moments praying for each other and for each of your spouses.

Before you begin this week's Video Teaching, pray for the Holy Spirit to come and bring revelation to your stand for restoration as you watch this week's teaching.

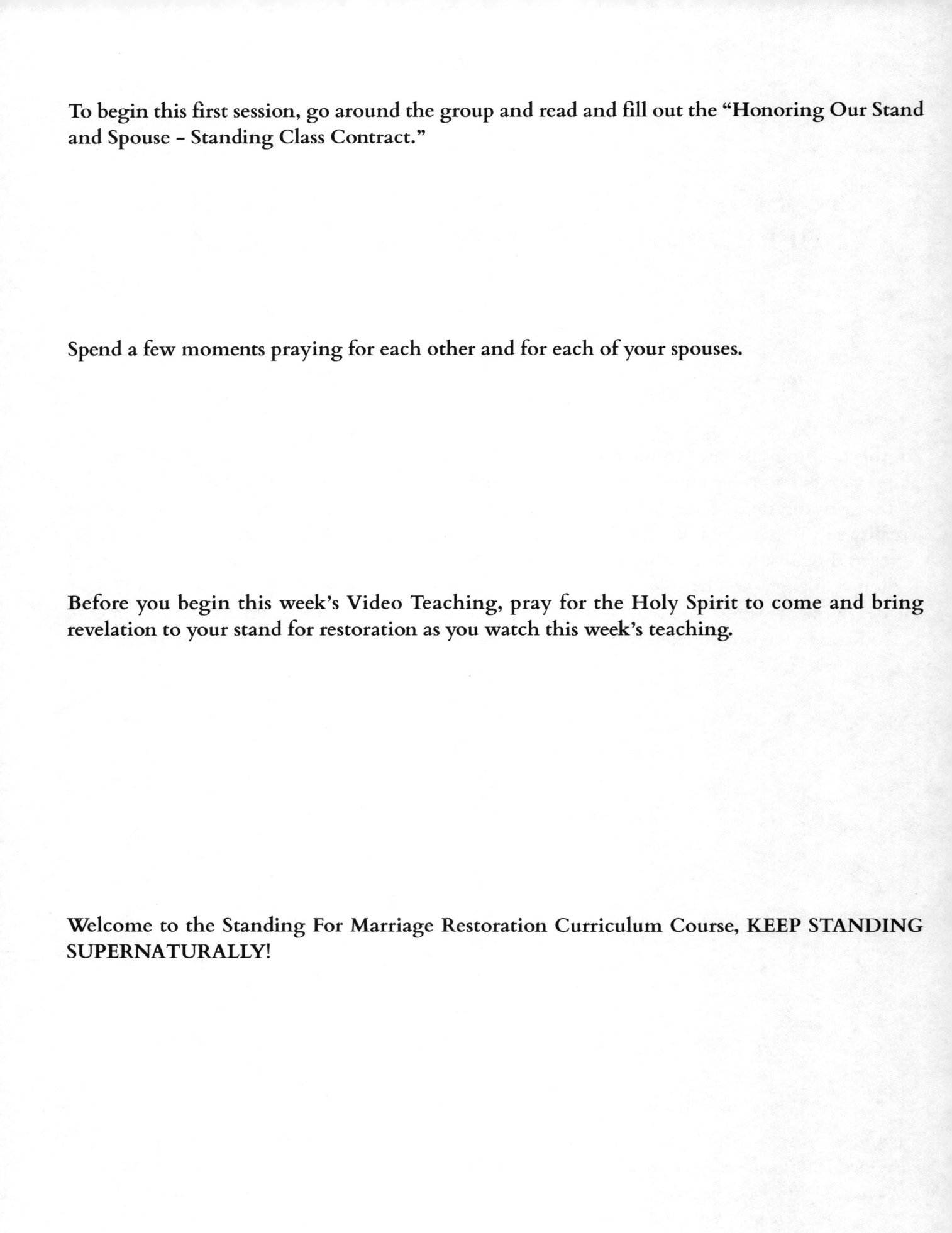

Welcome to the Standing For Marriage Restoration Curriculum Course, KEEP STANDING SUPERNATURALLY!

Follow along with this week's teaching video and fill in the blanks below as the answers appear on the screen.

Session 1 **VIDEO GUIDE** **STANDING FOR MARRIAGE RESTORATION**

1) God _____ restoring marriages even _____ separation or divorce.

2) Standing for your marriage isn't _____ the current reality of your marriage, but rather trusting in God's _____ to heal _____ the current brokenness in your marriage.

3) It's time we change the paradigm of how we think and talk about marriages from marriages constantly being in trouble, to something God is actively blessing, protecting, and even _____!

4) "You plus God makes the _____." - John Knox

5) We must never forget that _____ & _____ are at the core of the gospel! They are the very foundation of our faith.

6) The devil is actively trying to convince you that your _____ situation is more difficult than most and is probably too hard to be restored!

7) Make it your goal during this study to get to know and encounter the _____ of _____!

Discussion Questions from This Week's Teaching Video

Question #1: What part of Jason & Christine's marriage restoration testimony resonated most with you, and why?

Question #2: What does it mean to you to stand for your marriage without ignoring its current reality? How can you balance acknowledging the issues while still trusting in God's healing power?

Question #3: How do the actual divorce statistics presented in Shaunti Feldhahn's book "The Good News About Marriage" challenge the current perception of marriage? Does this encourage anyone to know that marriages are actually something God is blessing and protecting, and it is not as bad as it is being portrayed? Do you think this might be a plan of the enemy to spread these incorrect statistics?

Question #4: How does the concept of "You plus God make the majority" and the "Power of One" inspire your hope in your stand for marriage restoration? How can this belief empower your stand and how you think about what is possible?

Question #5: How can reminding yourself that the very foundation of the Gospel is that God is a restorer and that our entire religion is based on bringing things back from the dead impact your faith in your marriage restoration journey?

Question #6: Who here has thought and struggled with the belief that your specific situation is more difficult than most? You have faith for other marriages to be restored, but you often believe yours is probably harder than other people's. Can you now begin to see this is just a tactic of the enemy to get you to give up and that yours is NOT harder for God; the devil just wants you to believe that?

Question #7: Read Romans 15:13... How much do you think your stand can change if, during these next few weeks, you have a true encounter with the God of Hope? What does this verse say will come to you as you encounter the God of Hope?

This Week's Memory Verse

- **Jeremiah 32:27 (NIV)** *"I am the Lord, the God of all mankind. Is anything too hard for me?"*

- *(Bonus Memory Verse)* – **Romans 15:13 (NIV)** *"May the God of hope fill you with all joy and peace as you trust in him, so that you may overflow with hope by the power of the Holy Spirit."*

This Week's Daily Readings from "40 Day Stand for Marriage Restoration"

- **Day 1:** "DAY 1 – NOTHING IS IMPOSSIBLE" (Pages 4 – 11)

- **Day 2:** "DAY 2 – START WITH ME!" (Pages 12 – 20)

- **Day 3:** "DAY 3 – WONDERS THAT CANNOT BE FATHOMED" (Pages 21 – 27)

- **Day 4:** "DAY 4 – IS ANYTHING TOO HARD FOR HIM?" (Pages 28 – 34)

- **Day 5:** "DAY 5 – DON'T WAIT ON A WORD FOR YOUR MIRACLE!" (Pages 35 – 42)

Scriptures From This Week's Video Teaching

Luke 1:37 (ESV) "For nothing will be impossible with God."

Job 9:10 (NIV) "He performs wonders that cannot be fathomed, miracles that cannot be counted."

Matthew 19:5–6 (ESV) "⁵and said, 'Therefore a man shall leave his father and his mother and hold fast to his wife, and the two shall become one flesh'? ⁶So they are no longer two but one flesh. What therefore God has joined together, let not man separate."

Hebrews 11:1 (NIV) "Now faith is confidence in what we hope for and assurance about what we do not see."

Joel 2:25–26 (ESV) "²⁵I will restore to you the years that the swarming locust has eaten, the hopper, the destroyer, and the cutter, my great army, which I sent among you. ²⁶"You shall eat in plenty and be satisfied, and praise the name of the Lord your God, who has dealt wondrously with you. And my people shall never again be put to shame.

Lamentations 5:21 (NIV) "Restore us to yourself, Lord, that we may return; renew our days as of old."

Jeremiah 30:17 (NIV) "But I will restore you to health and heal your wounds,' declares the Lord, 'because you are called an outcast, Zion for whom no one cares.'"

1 Peter 5:10 (NIV) "And the God of all grace, who called you to his eternal glory in Christ, after you have suffered a little while, will himself restore you and make you strong, firm and steadfast."

Zechariah 9:12 (NIV) "Return to your fortress, you prisoners of hope; even now I announce that I will restore twice as much to you."

Ezekiel 36:26 (NIV) "I will give you a new heart and put a new spirit in you; I will remove from you your heart of stone and give you a heart of flesh."

Psalm 147:3 (NIV) "He heals the brokenhearted and binds up their wounds."

Jeremiah 32:27 (NIV) "I am the LORD, the God of all mankind. Is anything too hard for me?"

Romans 15:13 (NIV) "May the God of hope fill you with all joy and peace as you trust in him, so that you may overflow with hope by the power of the Holy Spirit."

SESSION 1 - DAY 1

DAY 1 – NOTHING IS IMPOSSIBLE

Luke 1:37 – "For nothing will be impossible with God."

Read pages 4 – 11: *Day 1 –* **Nothing is Impossible** from "40 Day Stand For Marriage Restoration"

Stand on this truth:

Imagine the moment when an angel of the Lord appeared to Mary, bearing the incredible message of the virgin birth. Mary might have desired more details or explanations, but the angel's message was simple and powerful: "For nothing will be impossible with God." In essence, the angel was inviting Mary to trust in God's ability to do the impossible, regardless of how it seemed in the natural. Just like Mary, God invites you to believe in His supernatural power to fulfill His assignments in your life, particularly in restoring your marriage, even when it seems impossible. The circumstances, your emotions, and the opinions of others do not determine what God can and will do.

Prayer for Today:

"Father, today I ask that You open my eyes to Your limitless power. I believe in Your desire to restore my family, and I trust in Your Word. Remove any doubt and impart unwavering faith in Your ability to do the impossible, especially in restoring my marriage. Thank You, God, for being a God of restoration. In Jesus' name, I pray. Amen."

Activate Your Stand:

1. Ask the Holy Spirit to reveal how your stand can look when you firmly believe that **nothing is impossible with God.** Write down any insights or thoughts.

2. Identify and write down any lies from today's **"Lies to Reject"** that you've been struggling with. Cross them out symbolically to break their hold on your mind.

3. Write down below and begin to speak aloud a few of today's **"Daily Truths to Declare."** Believe that they are true and activated in your stand for restoration.

DAY 1 — "NOTHING IS IMPOSSIBLE"

Today's Verse: Luke 1:37

Today's Reading: Pages 4 - 11

Your Marriage IS Getting Restored!

Today's Coloring Page:

"From Coloring Your Stand" Coloring Book

Session 1 - Day 2

DAY 2 - START WITH ME

Psalm 139:23-24 (NIV): *"Search me, God, and know my heart; test me and know my anxious thoughts. See if there is any offensive way in me, and lead me in the way everlasting."*

Read pages 12 - 20: **Day 2 – Start With Me** from "40 Day Stand For Marriage Restoration"

Stand on this truth:

Starting with yourself: Acknowledge any offensive ways and embrace humility as you seek personal transformation in your stand for restoration. Join us today in self-reflection and surrender. Let's invite the Holy Spirit to search our hearts and reveal any areas in need of transformation. As we acknowledge our own shortcomings and embrace humility, we open the door for God's healing work in our lives and marriages. It's natural to focus on our spouse's actions and faults when standing for marriage restoration. However, today's devotion reminds us to begin with introspection. We're called to pray the prayer of Psalm 139:23-24, inviting the Holy Spirit to examine our hearts and reveal any areas where we may have contributed to the breakdown of our relationship.

Prayer for Today:

"Heavenly Father, I invite You to search my heart, know my thoughts, and reveal any areas that need transformation. Help me to acknowledge my shortcomings and approach reconciliation with humility. Guide me in the path of everlasting restoration. Amen."

Activate Today's Lesson:

1. How can confidently believing that **your restoration starts with you** impact your stand for marriage restoration?

2. Identify and write down any lies from today's **"Lies to Reject"** that you've been struggling with. Cross them out symbolically to break their hold on your mind.

3. Write down below and begin to speak aloud a few of today's **"Daily Truths to Declare."** Believe that they are true and activated in your stand for restoration.

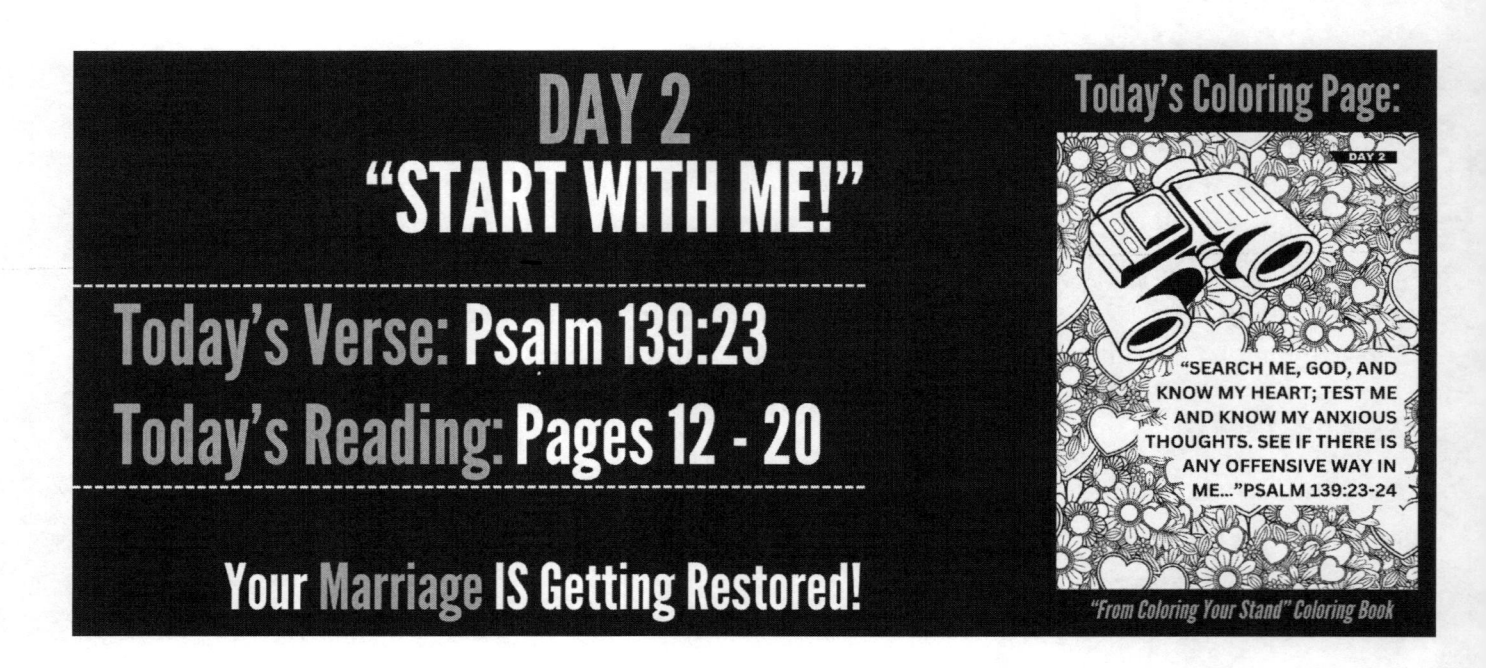

DAY 2
"START WITH ME!"

Today's Verse: Psalm 139:23
Today's Reading: Pages 12 - 20

Your Marriage IS Getting Restored!

Today's Coloring Page:

"SEARCH ME, GOD, AND KNOW MY HEART; TEST ME AND KNOW MY ANXIOUS THOUGHTS. SEE IF THERE IS ANY OFFENSIVE WAY IN ME..." PSALM 139:23-24

"From Coloring Your Stand" Coloring Book

Session 1 - Day 3

Day 3 – Wonders That Cannot Be Fathomed

Job 9:10 (NIV) "He performs wonders that cannot be fathomed, miracles that cannot be counted."

Read pages 21 – 27: **Day 3 – Wonders That Cannot Be Fathomed** from "40 Day Stand For Marriage Restoration"

Stand on this truth:

Embracing the miraculous: Recognize God's ability to perform wonders beyond your comprehension as you stand in faith for restoration. Let's surrender our need for understanding and trust in His ability to bring about restoration that surpasses our expectations. In the midst of our marital challenges, it's easy to become overwhelmed by the complexities of our situations. However, Job 9:10 reminds us that God's wonders are beyond our comprehension. Today, let's release our need to understand and embrace the miraculous work of God in our lives.

Prayer for Today:

"Heavenly Father, I acknowledge Your limitless power and authority. Help me to release my need for understanding and surrender to Your plan for my marriage. I trust in Your miraculous work and believe in Your abundance. Guide me as I stand in faith for restoration. Amen."

Activate Today's Lesson:

1. How can embracing the **miraculous nature of God's power** impact your stand for marriage restoration?

2. Identify and write down any lies from today's **"Lies to Reject"** that you've been struggling with. Cross them out symbolically to break their hold on your mind.

3. Write down below and begin to speak aloud a few of today's **"Daily Truths to Declare."** Believe that they are true and activated in your stand for restoration.

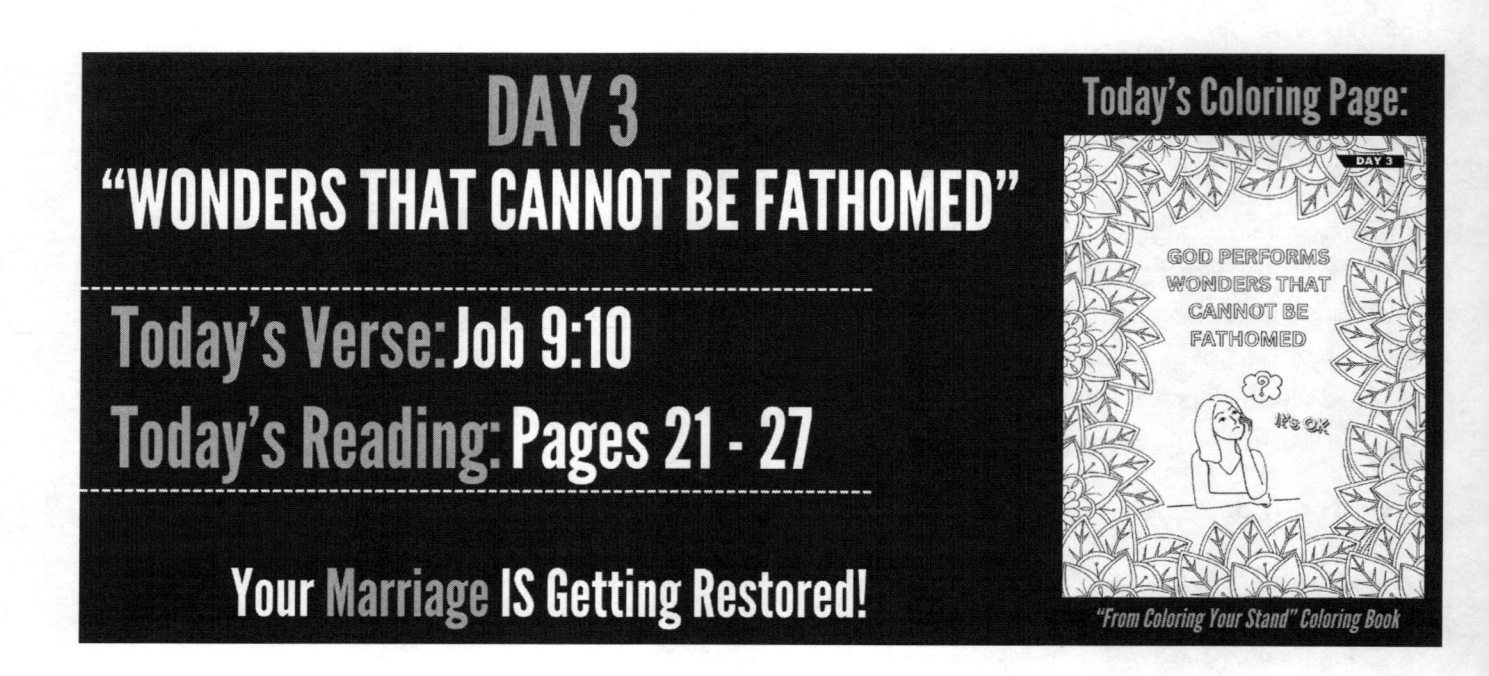

DAY 3
"WONDERS THAT CANNOT BE FATHOMED"

Today's Verse: **Job 9:10**

Today's Reading: **Pages 21 - 27**

Your Marriage IS Getting Restored!

Today's Coloring Page:

"From Coloring Your Stand" Coloring Book

Session 1 - Day 4

Day 4: Is Anything Too Hard for Him?

Jeremiah 32:27 (NIV) "I am the LORD, the God of all mankind. Is anything too hard for me?"

Read pages 28 - 34: **Day 4: Is Anything Too Hard for Him?** from "40 Day Stand For Marriage Restoration"

Stand on this truth:

Is anything too hard for Him? Let's delve into Jeremiah 32:27 and reflect on the assurance that God's power transcends any challenge we face in our marriages. Join us today in pondering the question posed by God Himself: "Is anything too hard for me?" Let's set aside our doubts and fears and invite the Holy Spirit to illuminate the truth of God's limitless power in our hearts. It's natural to wrestle with doubts, especially when faced with the daunting task of restoring a marriage. However, today's passage reminds us that God's power knows no bounds. He reigns over all mankind, and there is nothing too difficult for Him to accomplish.

Prayer for Today:

"Heavenly Father, I come before You acknowledging any doubts or fears I may have about Your ability to restore my marriage. Help me to trust in Your sovereignty and to believe wholeheartedly that nothing is too hard for You. Forgive me for any unbelief, and strengthen my faith as I stand for restoration. In Jesus' name, amen."

Activate Today's Lesson:

1. How does the assurance that **nothing is too hard for God** impact your perspective on marriage restoration?

2. Identify and write down any lies from today's **"Lies to Reject"** that you've been struggling with. Cross them out symbolically to break their hold on your mind.

3. Write down below and begin to speak aloud a few of today's **"Daily Truths to Declare."** Believe that they are true and activated in your stand for restoration.

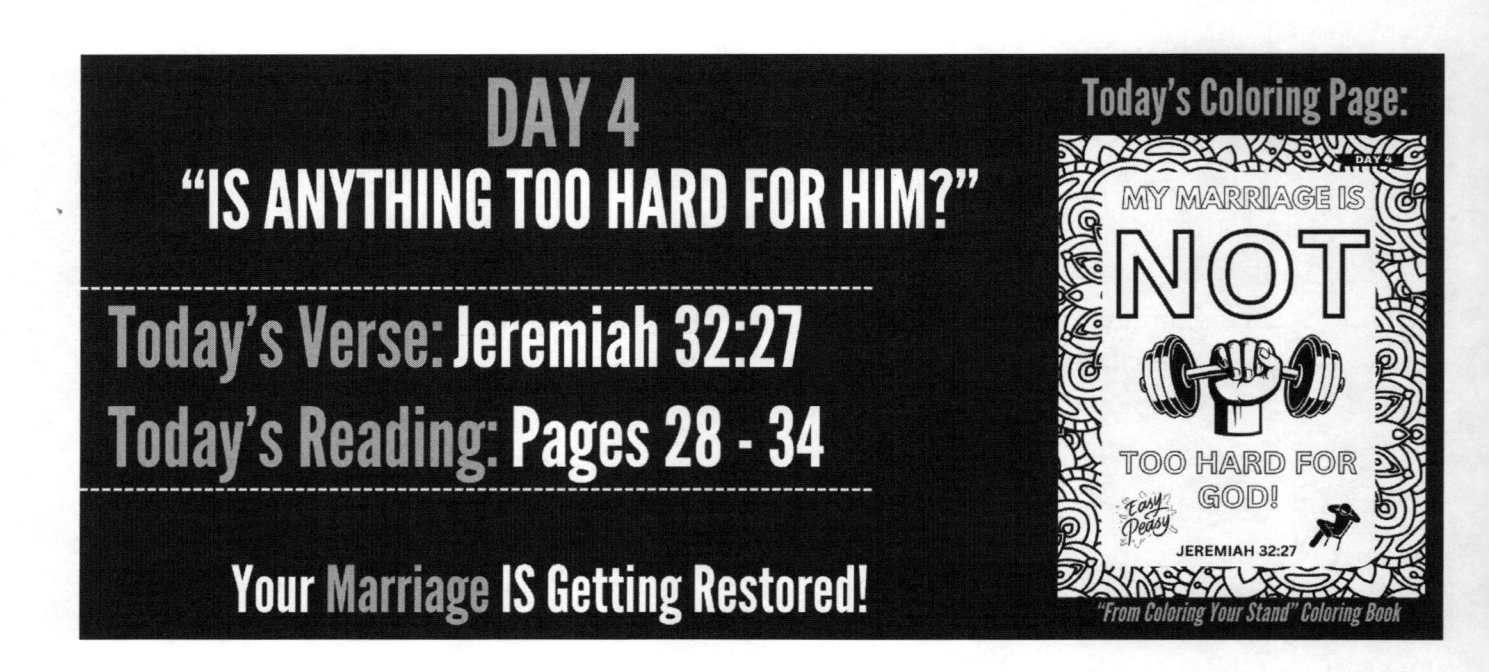

DAY 4
"IS ANYTHING TOO HARD FOR HIM?"

Today's Verse: Jeremiah 32:27
Today's Reading: Pages 28 - 34

Your Marriage IS Getting Restored!

Today's Coloring Page:
MY MARRIAGE IS NOT TOO HARD FOR GOD!
JEREMIAH 32:27
"From Coloring Your Stand" Coloring Book

Session 1 - Day 5

Day 5: Don't Wait on a Word for Your Miracle!

Luke 8:44 (TPT): *"Pressing in through the crowd, she came up behind Jesus and touched the tassel of his prayer shawl. Instantly her bleeding stopped and she was healed."*

Read pages 35 – 42: DAY 5 – DON'T WAIT ON A WORD FOR YOUR MIRACLE! Day Stand For Marriage Restoration"

Stand on this truth:

Don't Wait on a Word for Your Miracle! Let's delve into Luke 8:44 and reflect on the powerful story of the woman who reached out in faith to touch the hem of Jesus' garment for her divine healing. In the story of the woman with the issue of blood, we witness a remarkable display of faith. Despite not receiving a specific word or promise from God, she chose to act in faith, believing in the power of Jesus to heal her. This story reminds us that we don't always need a direct word to believe in God's ability to work miracles in our lives.

Prayer for Today:

"Heavenly Father, as I stand for the restoration of my marriage, I come before You in faith, just like the woman who touched the hem of Jesus' garment. Even when I don't have a specific word or promise, I trust in Your power and goodness. Help me, Lord, to keep my faith anchored in You, knowing that Your ways are higher than my ways. May my faith-filled actions be the catalyst for a miraculous restoration in my marriage."

Activate Today's Lesson:

1. How does the story of <u>**the woman with the issue of blood**</u> inspire your faith in God's power to restore marriages?

2. Identify and write down any lies from today's <u>**"Lies to Reject"**</u> that you've been struggling with. Cross them out symbolically to break their hold on your mind.

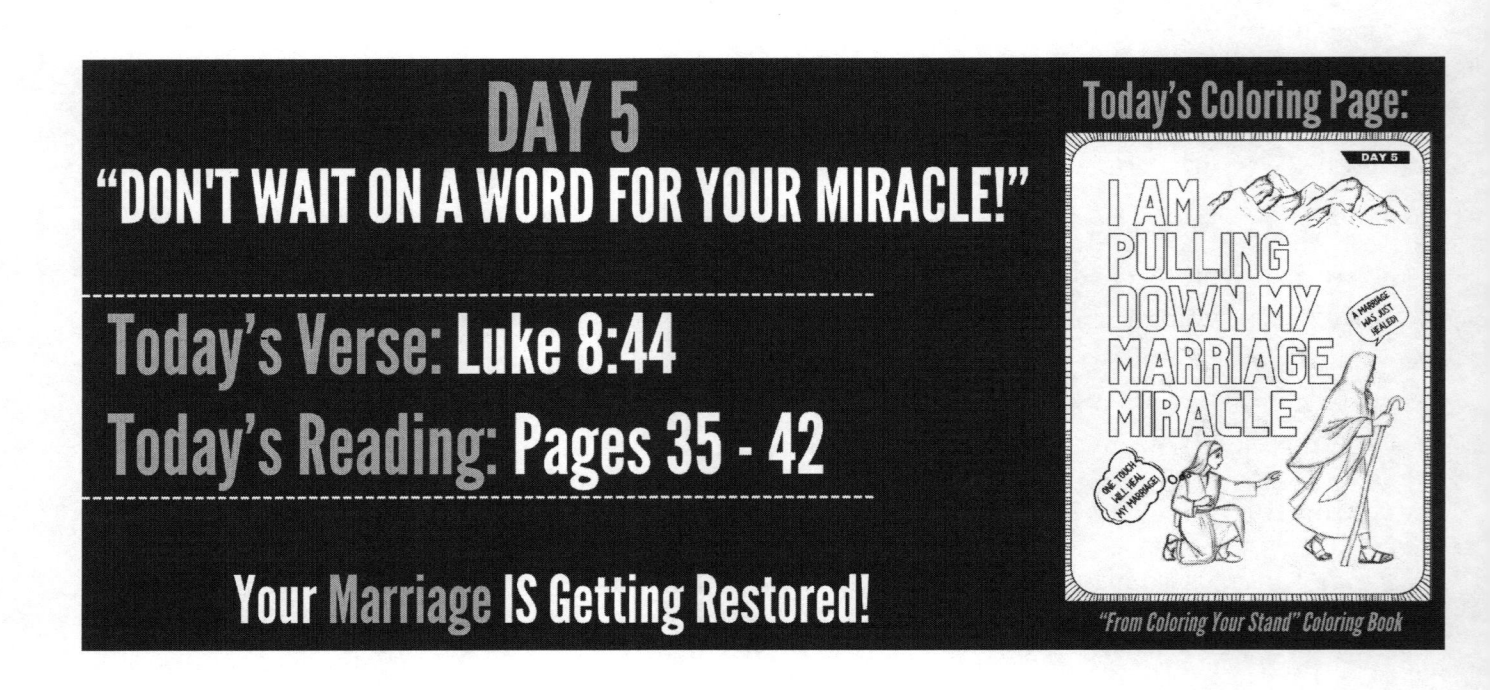

3. Write down below and begin to speak aloud a few of today's <u>**"Daily Truths to Declare."**</u> Believe that they are true and activated in your stand for restoration.

DAY 5
"DON'T WAIT ON A WORD FOR YOUR MIRACLE!"

Today's Verse: **Luke 8:44**
Today's Reading: **Pages 35 - 42**

Your Marriage IS Getting Restored!

Today's Coloring Page:

I AM PULLING DOWN MY MARRIAGE MIRACLE
A MARRIAGE HAS JUST HEALED
ONE TOUCH WILL HEAL MY MARRIAGE!
DAY 5

"From Coloring Your Stand" Coloring Book

SESSION 1 - DAY 6

REVIEWING THIS WEEK'S DAILY READINGS

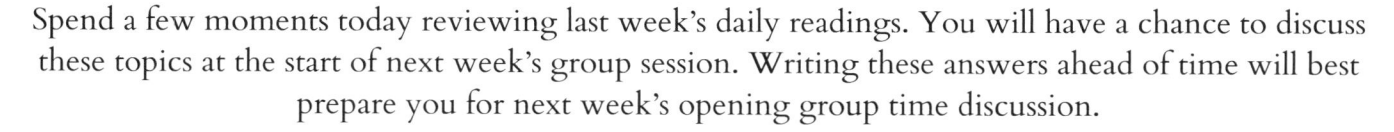

Spend a few moments today reviewing last week's daily readings. You will have a chance to discuss these topics at the start of next week's group session. Writing these answers ahead of time will best prepare you for next week's opening group time discussion.

What encouraging takeaways did you have from this day's reading? What specific thoughts, verses, lies, declarations, or testimonies are specifically impactful for your stand?

Day 1 – "Day 1: Nothing is Impossible" insights:

Day 2 – "Day 2: Start with Me" insights:

Day 3 – "Day 3: Wonders That Cannot Be Fathomed" insights:

Day 4 – "Day 4: Is Anything Too Hard for Him?" insights:

Day 5 – "Day 5: Don't Wait on a Word for Your Miracle!" insights:

Write this week's Memory Verse below:

Additional Notes:

SESSION 2 - SPIRITUAL WARFARE OVER MARRIAGES

In this session, "Spiritual Warfare Over Marriages," Pastor Jason Carver reveals that the struggles in your marriage are not merely relational but part of a greater spiritual battle. Drawing from Ephesians 6:12, he emphasizes that your spouse is not the enemy; rather, the devil is working to bring destruction to marriages because they reflect Christ's love for the Church. You will learn how to identify and stand firm against the enemy's tactics, use God's Word as your weapon, and exercise the spiritual authority Jesus has given you. This session equips you to fight for your marriage through prayer, worship, and trust in God's power to destroy the works of the devil.

"A primary tactic of the enemy is to blind the minds of both the spouse and the one standing for their marriage to be restored. Making them unable to see the hope and potential in their marriage. But Jesus came to destroy the works of the devil, and with His power, we can overcome all the enemy's schemes." – Jason Carver

Discussion and review from last week's daily readings of "40 Day Stand For Marriage Restoration."

Before you begin this week's teaching video, go around the group and discuss your insights and takeaways from each of the daily readings from last week. Revisit last week's Day 6 Workbook page for an overview of your reading takeaways.

Write any insights from other group members below:

Any specific day from last week's reading that you need to go back and read again?

Before you begin this week's Video Teaching, pray for the Holy Spirit to come and bring revelation to your stand for restoration as you watch this week's teaching.

Follow along with this week's teaching video and fill in the blanks below as the answers appear on the screen.

Session 2 **VIDEO GUIDE** **STANDING FOR MARRIAGE RESTORATION**

1) Marriage is a _____ picture of Jesus and His love for the church. By attacking marriages, the devil aims to attack Jesus. The devil can't destroy Jesus, so he is trying to destroy what Jesus _____.

2) There is a _____ war going on over your marriage!

3) Your marriage battle is not against your _____ but against the _____ forces coming against you both.

4) If you are going to stand for your marriage you must become _____ with and no longer oblivious to the _____ of the _____.

5) The enemy is actively trying to _____ the _____ of our spouses so they no longer _____ and can't _____ anything good in the marriage.

6) Jesus' mission was to _____ all the works of the devil, and that includes the devil's work against your _____.

7) _____ have been authorized by Jesus to trample on the demonic influences against your marriage and _____ all the powers of the enemy.

Discussion Questions from This Week's Teaching Video

Question #1: What do you think about the idea that the devil attacks marriage because marriage is a picture of Jesus' love for the church and the devil is trying to attack Jesus?

Question #2: Have you ever thought the issues surrounding your marriage are not merely relational disagreements but actually have a spiritual warfare component to it?

Question #3: Reflecting on Ephesians 6:12, how can recognizing this is a spiritual battle help you approach conflicts and challenges with your spouse differently? How can you remind yourself that your spouse is not the enemy?

Question #4: Why is it crucial to be aware of the devil's schemes when standing for your marriage? Can you identify any specific tactics the enemy has used against your relationship, and how can you counteract them?

Question #5: Do you believe the enemy is trying to blind the mind of your spouse so they cannot see what is good about your marriage? What can you do to combat this blinding and help restore your spouse's vision of the positive aspects of your relationship?

Question #6: How does knowing that Jesus came to destroy the works of the devil, including attacks on your marriage, encourage you? What promises from Jesus can you hold onto during this battle?

Question #7: Jesus has authorized you to trample on demonic influences and overcome the enemy. How can you practically exercise this authority in your marriage?

This Week's Memory Verse

- *Ephesians 6:12 (NIV)* "For our struggle is not against flesh and blood, but against the rulers, against the authorities, against the powers of this dark world and against the spiritual forces of evil in the heavenly realms."

- **(Bonus Memory Verse)** – *1 John 3:8b (NIV)* "The reason the Son of God appeared was to destroy the devil's work."

This Week's Daily Readings from "40 Day Stand for Marriage Restoration"

- **Day 1:** "DAY 6 – JESUS CAME TO DESTROY" (Pages 43 – 49)
- **Day 2:** "DAY 7 – NOT OBLIVIOUS TO THE WAYS OF THE DEVIL" (Pages 50 – 57)
- **Day 3:** "DAY 12 – WALK IN YOUR DEAD-RAISING AUTHORITY" (Pages 82 – 89)
- **Day 4:** "DAY 20 – KNOW YOUR REAL ENEMY" (Pages 149 – 155)
- **Day 5:** DAY 24 – "PEACE IS A WEAPON" (Pages 178 – 185)

Scriptures From This Week's Video Teaching

John 10:10 (NIV) "The thief comes only to steal and kill and destroy; I have come that they may have life, and have it to the full."

Ephesians 5:31-32 (NIV) "For this reason a man will leave his father and mother and be united to his wife, and the two will become one flesh. This is a profound mystery—but I am talking about Christ and the church."

1 Peter 5:8 (NIV) "Be alert and of sober mind. Your enemy the devil prowls around like a roaring lion looking for someone to devour."

Ephesians 6:12 (NIV) "For our struggle is not against flesh and blood, but against the rulers, against the authorities, against the powers of this dark world and against the spiritual forces of evil in the heavenly realms."

2 Corinthians 2:11 (NLT) "So that Satan will not outsmart us. For we are familiar with his evil schemes."

2 Corinthians 2:11 (MSG) "After all, we don't want to unwittingly give Satan an opening for yet more mischief; we are not oblivious to his sly ways."

2 Corinthians 4:4 (NIV) "The god of this age has blinded the minds of unbelievers, so that they cannot see the light of the gospel that displays the glory of Christ, who is the image of God."

2 Corinthians 4:4 (TPT) "For their minds have been blinded by the god of this age, leaving them in unbelief. Their blindness keeps them from seeing the dayspring light of the wonderful news of the glory of Jesus Christ, who is the divine image of God."

1 John 3:8 (NIV): "The reason the Son of God appeared was to destroy the devil's work."

Luke 10:19 (NIV) "I have given you authority to trample on snakes and scorpions and to overcome all the power of the enemy; nothing will harm you."

Romans 16:20 (NIV) "The God of peace will soon crush Satan under your feet. The grace of our Lord Jesus be with you."

Session 2 - Day 1

Day 6: Jesus Came to Destroy!

1 John 3:8b (ESV) "The reason the Son of God appeared was to destroy the works of the devil."

Read pages 43 - 49: *Day 6: Jesus Came to Destroy!* from "40 Day Stand For Marriage Restoration."

Stand on this truth:

Jesus came to destroy! Let's explore 1 John 3:8b and reflect on how Jesus' mission to destroy the works of the devil applies to our marriages. Jesus' purpose on Earth was not only to bring peace and harmony but also to confront and destroy the works of the devil. This includes the destructive forces that seek to tear apart marriages, such as divorce, separation, adultery, and hardness of heart.

Prayer for Today:

"Heavenly Father, thank you for the profound truth revealed in 1 John 3:8 that Jesus came to destroy the works of the devil. I lift up the brokenness and strife in my marriage, recognizing them as the works of the enemy. I trust in Your sovereign plan and stand with unwavering faith, believing that my marriage is a testament to Jesus' mission of destruction. May Your will be done, and may Your glory shine through the restoration of my marriage. In Jesus' name, amen."

Activate Today's Lesson:

1. How does the truth that **Jesus came to destroy** the works of the devil impact your perspective on marriage restoration?

2. Identify and write down any lies from today's **"Lies to Reject"** that you've been struggling with. Cross them out symbolically to break their hold on your mind.

3. Write down below and begin to speak aloud a few of today's **"Daily Truths to Declare."** Believe that they are true and activated in your stand for restoration.

DAY 6
"JESUS CAME TO DESTROY!"

Today's Verse: **1 John 3:8**
Today's Reading: **Pages 43 - 49**

Your Marriage IS Getting Restored!

Today's Coloring Page:
"From Coloring Your Stand" Coloring Book

Session 2 - Day 2

Day 7: Not Oblivious to the Ways of the Devil

2 Corinthians 2:11 (The Message) "After all, we don't want to unwittingly give Satan an opening for yet more mischief—we're not oblivious to his sly ways!"

Read pages 50 - 57: <u>*Day 7: Not Oblivious to the Ways of the Devil*</u> from "40 Day Stand For Marriage Restoration."

Stand on this truth:

In the battle for marriage restoration, ignorance is not bliss. The devil operates in sly ways, seeking to exploit our vulnerabilities and catch us off guard. However, as believers, we are not ignorant of his schemes. Just as a football team studies their opponent's plays to gain an advantage, we must understand the devil's strategies to stand strong in the face of adversity.

Prayer for Today:

"Heavenly Father, thank you for revealing in 2 Corinthians 2:11 that we are not to be ignorant of the enemy's tactics. Grant me the insight to recognize the devil's cunning ways and stand firm in the light of Your truth. Guide me to navigate the path to marriage restoration with confidence, knowing that victory is assured by You. In Jesus' name, amen."

Activate Today's Lesson:

1. How does being <u>**aware of the devil's tactics**</u> impact your perspective on marriage restoration?

2. Identify and write down any lies from today's <u>**"Lies to Reject"**</u> that you've been struggling with. Cross them out symbolically to break their hold on your mind.

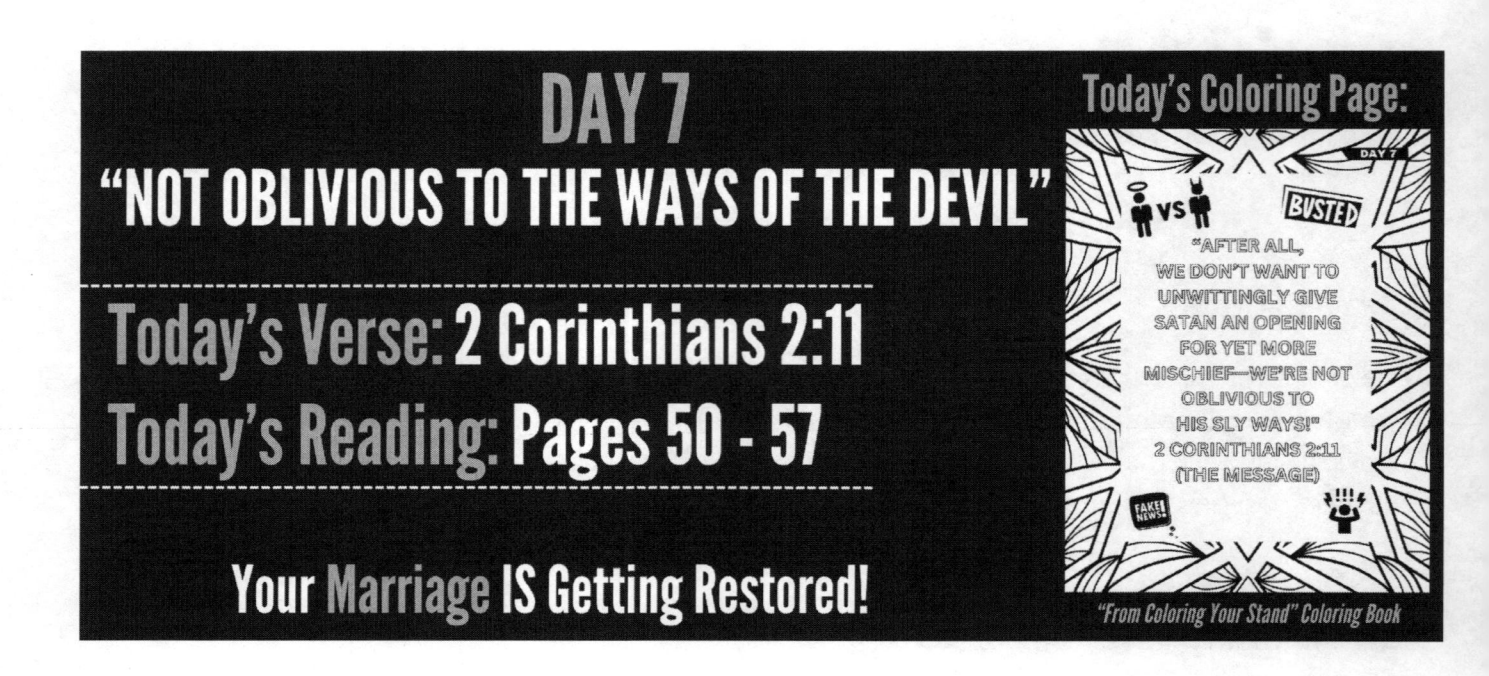

3. Write down below and begin to speak aloud a few of today's <u>**"Daily Truths to Declare."**</u> Believe that they are true and activated in your stand for restoration.

DAY 7
"NOT OBLIVIOUS TO THE WAYS OF THE DEVIL"

Today's Verse: 2 Corinthians 2:11
Today's Reading: Pages 50 - 57

Your Marriage IS Getting Restored!

Today's Coloring Page:

"AFTER ALL, WE DON'T WANT TO UNWITTINGLY GIVE SATAN AN OPENING FOR YET MORE MISCHIEF—WE'RE NOT OBLIVIOUS TO HIS SLY WAYS!"
2 CORINTHIANS 2:11
(THE MESSAGE)

"From Coloring Your Stand" Coloring Book

Session 2 - Day 3

Day 12: Walking in Your Dead-Raising Authority

Matthew 10:8 (NIV) "Heal the sick, raise the dead, cleanse those who have leprosy, drive out demons. Freely you have received, freely give."

Read pages 90 - 97: **Day 12: Walking in Your Dead-Raising Authority** from "40 Day Stand For Marriage Restoration."

Stand on this truth:

Walking in your dead-raising authority! Let's delve into Matthew 10:8 and understand how this verse speaks to the supernatural authority given to believers and its relevance to marriage restoration. Understanding the authority bestowed upon us by Jesus is crucial as we stand for the restoration of our marriages. Jesus empowered His disciples—and us—with the authority to heal, raise the dead, cleanse, and drive out demons. This authority is not merely historical; it's a living mandate for us today.

Prayer for Today:

"Heavenly Father, as I stand for the restoration of my marriage, I recognize the authority You have given me to heal, raise what is dead, and cast out any demonic oppression hindering reconciliation. Guide me by Your Holy Spirit as I walk in this authority, trusting in Your resurrection power to breathe life back into my marriage. May Your anointing flow through me to bring healing, restoration, and wholeness to my relationship. In Jesus' name, amen."

Activate Today's Lesson:

1. How does the mandate of **Matthew 10:8** impact your perspective on marriage restoration?

2. Identify and write down any lies from today's **"Lies to Reject"** that you've been struggling with. Cross them out symbolically to break their hold on your mind.

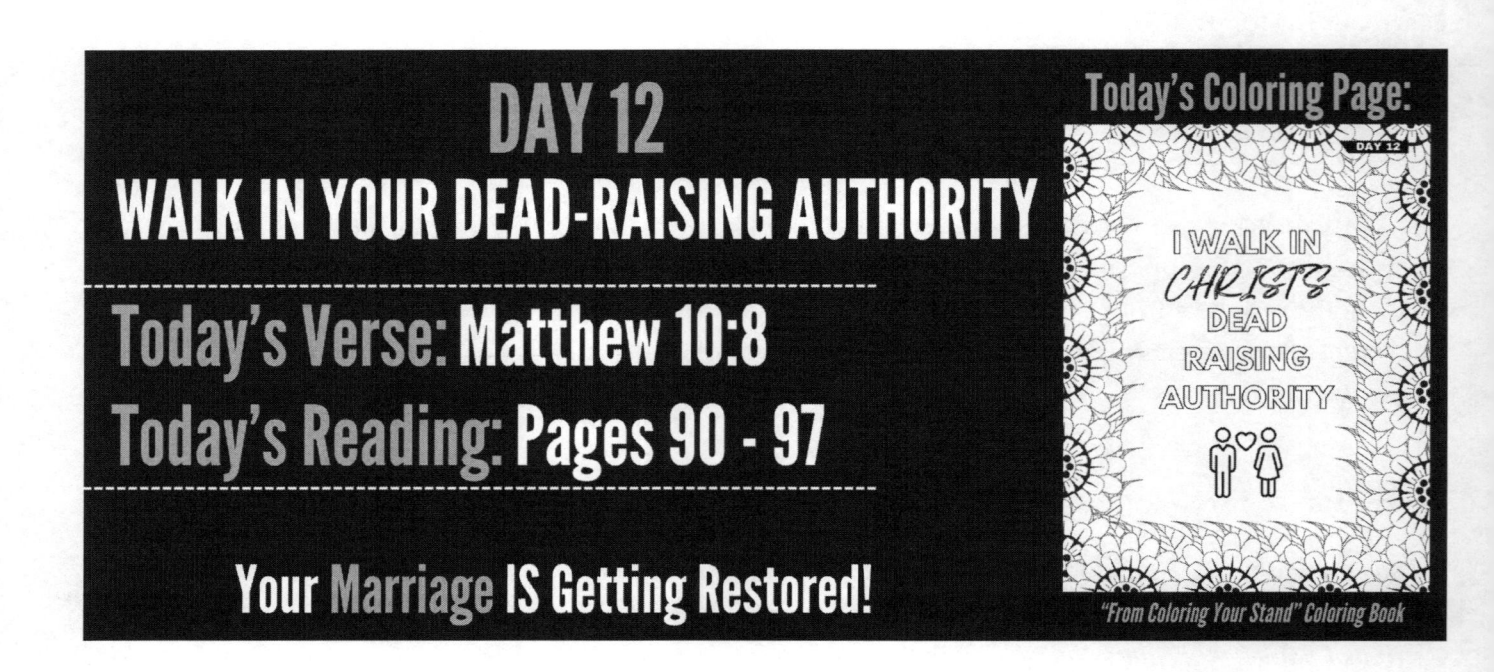

3. Write down below and begin to speak aloud a few of today's **"Daily Truths to Declare."** Believe that they are true and activated in your stand for restoration.

DAY 12
WALK IN YOUR DEAD-RAISING AUTHORITY

Today's Verse: Matthew 10:8
Today's Reading: Pages 90 - 97

Your Marriage IS Getting Restored!

Today's Coloring Page:
I WALK IN CHRIST'S DEAD RAISING AUTHORITY

"From Coloring Your Stand" Coloring Book

Session 2 - Day 4

Day 20: Know Your Real Enemy

Ephesians 6:12 (NIV) "For our struggle is not against flesh and blood, but against the rulers, against the authorities, against the powers of this dark world and against the spiritual forces of evil in the heavenly realms."

Read pages 149 – 155: *Day 20: Know Your Real Enemy* from "40 Day Stand For Marriage Restoration."

Stand on this truth:

In the midst of marital challenges, it's essential to recognize that our true enemy is not our spouse but the spiritual forces of evil seeking to destroy God's design for marriage. Do you find yourself directing your frustration and anger toward your spouse amidst marital difficulties? Ephesians 6:12 reminds us that our battle is not against our spouse but against spiritual forces at work.

Prayer for Today:

"Heavenly Father, I acknowledge that my battle is not against my spouse but against the spiritual forces at work. Help me discern the enemy's schemes and stand firm in the authority I have in Christ. Fill me with compassion, love, and grace for my spouse, even during challenges. Grant me wisdom and strength as I wage war through prayer. In Jesus' name, amen."

Activate Today's Lesson:

1. How can you shift your focus today from **viewing your spouse as the enemy** to recognizing the true spiritual battle?

2. Identify and write down any lies from today's **"Lies to Reject"** that you've been struggling with. Cross them out symbolically to break their hold on your mind.

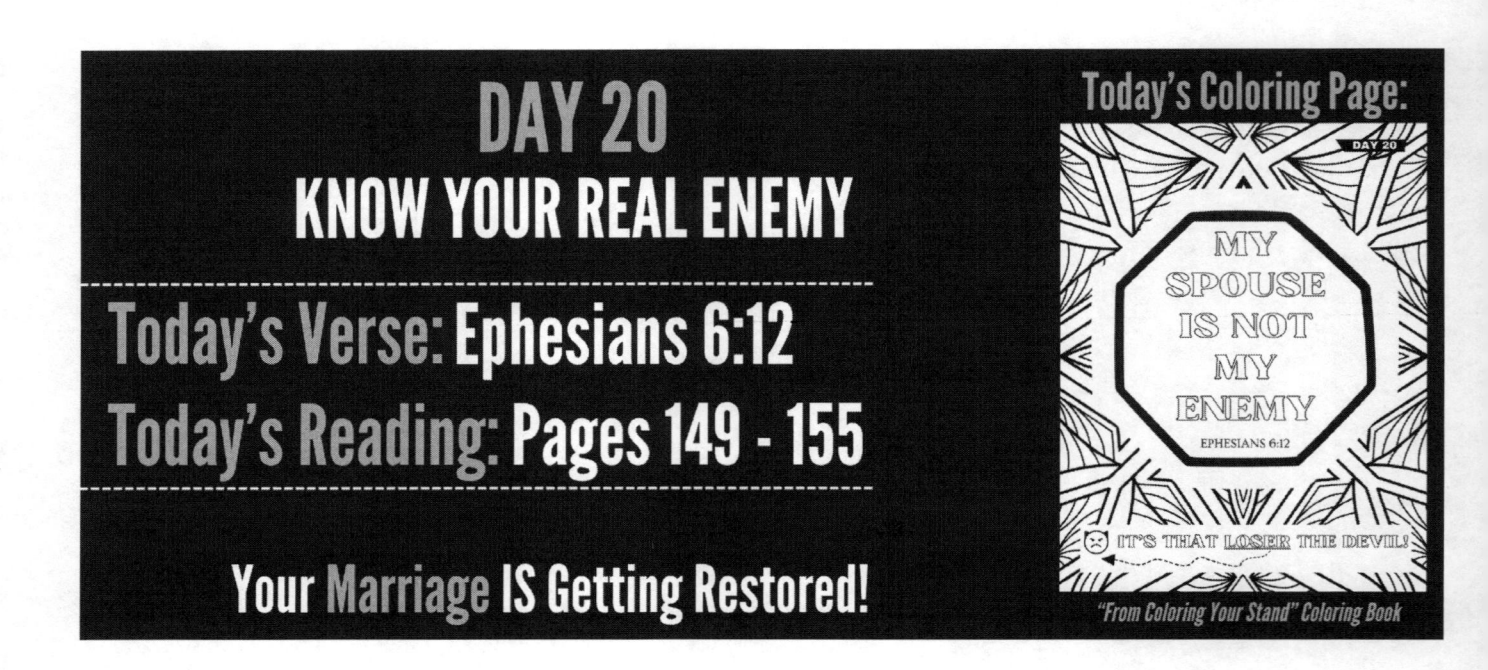

3. Write down below and begin to speak aloud a few of today's **"Daily Truths to Declare."** Believe that they are true and activated in your stand for restoration.

DAY 20
KNOW YOUR REAL ENEMY

Today's Verse: **Ephesians 6:12**
Today's Reading: **Pages 149 - 155**

Your Marriage IS Getting Restored!

Today's Coloring Page:

MY SPOUSE IS NOT MY ENEMY
EPHESIANS 6:12

IT'S THAT LOSER THE DEVIL!

"From Coloring Your Stand" Coloring Book

Session 2 - Day 5

Day 24: Peace is a Weapon!

Romans 16:20 (ESV) "The God of peace will soon crush Satan under your feet. The grace of our Lord Jesus Christ be with you."

Read pages 178 – 185: *Day 24: Peace is a Weapon!* from "40 Day Stand For Marriage Restoration."

Stand on this truth:

Even though it may seem unusual to consider peace as a weapon, Romans 16:20 assures us that the God of peace will crush Satan under our feet. This verse highlights the active role of peace in our spiritual warfare. Peace is not merely a passive state of tranquility but a supernatural weapon that disarms the enemy and paves the way for God's victory to manifest in our marriages.

Prayer for Today:

"Heavenly Father, I thank You for being the God of peace who crushes Satan under my feet. Help me fully grasp the power of peace as a supernatural weapon in the spiritual realm. Guide me in actively pursuing peace in my thoughts, words, and actions, especially in the midst of marital challenges. May Your peace guard my heart and mind, enabling me to respond to my spouse with love, grace, and wisdom. I surrender my marriage to You, trusting in Your supernatural intervention to bring restoration and reconciliation. In Jesus' name, amen."

Activate Today's Lesson:

1. Reflect on the **power of peace as a spiritual weapon** in your marriage. How could embracing this truth impact your stand for restoration??

2. Identify and write down any lies from today's **"Lies to Reject"** that you've been struggling with. Cross them out symbolically to break their hold on your mind.

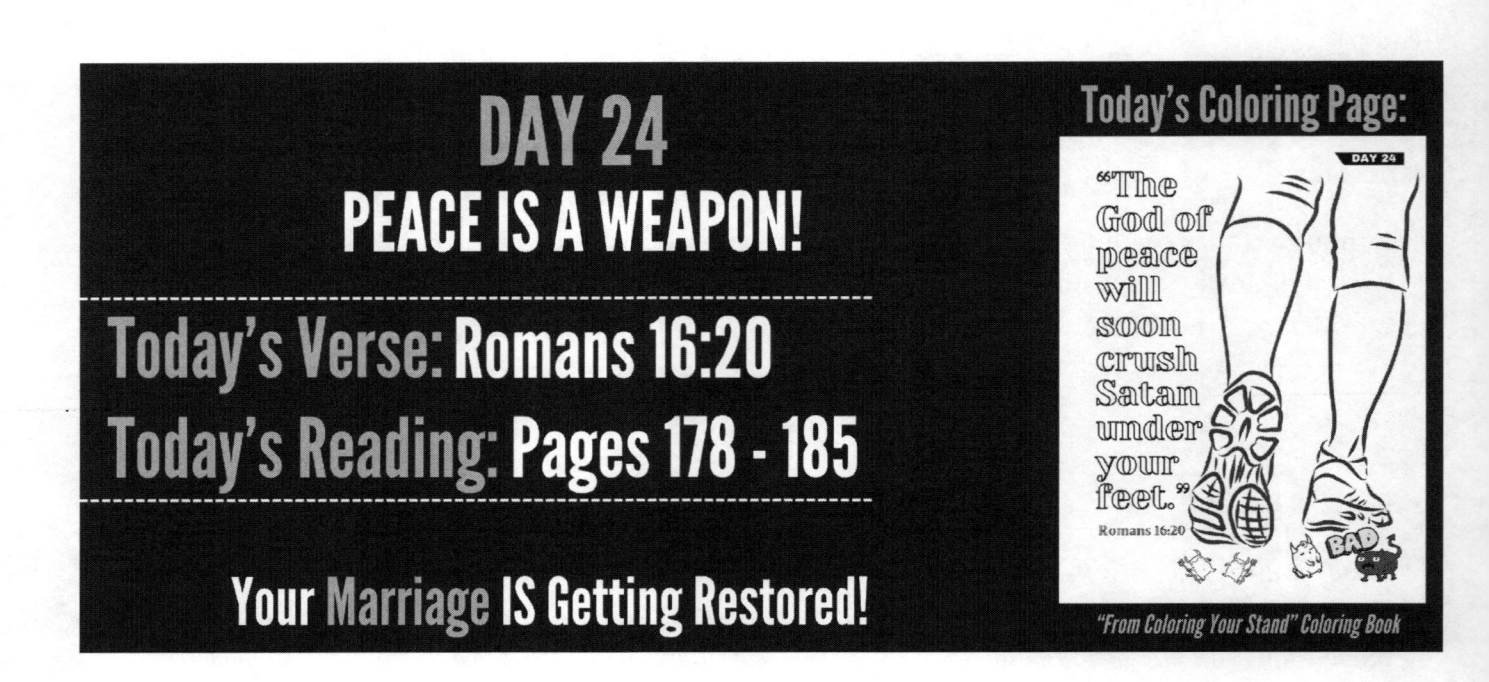

3. Write down below and begin to speak aloud a few of today's **"Daily Truths to Declare."** Believe that they are true and activated in your stand for restoration.

DAY 24
PEACE IS A WEAPON!

Today's Verse: **Romans 16:20**
Today's Reading: **Pages 178 - 185**

Your Marriage IS Getting Restored!

Today's Coloring Page:

"The God of peace will soon crush Satan under your feet." Romans 16:20

"From Coloring Your Stand" Coloring Book

SESSION 2 - DAY 6

REVIEWING THIS WEEK'S DAILY READINGS

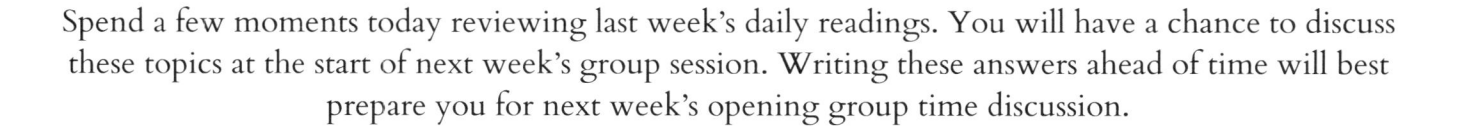

Spend a few moments today reviewing last week's daily readings. You will have a chance to discuss these topics at the start of next week's group session. Writing these answers ahead of time will best prepare you for next week's opening group time discussion.

What encouraging takeaways did you have from this day's reading? What specific thoughts, verses, lies, declarations, or testimonies are specifically impactful for your stand?

Day 1 – "Day 6: Jesus Came to Destroy!" insights:

Day 2 – "Day 7: Not Oblivious to the Ways of the Devil!" insights:

Day 3 – "Day 12: Walking in Your Dead-Raising Authority" insights:

Day 4 – "Day 20: Know Your Real Enemy" insights:

Day 5 – "Day 24: Peace is a Weapon!" insights:

Write this week's Memory Verse below:

Additional Notes:

SESSION 3 - RECONCILIATION AND REPENTANCE

In session 3, "Reconciliation and Repentance," Pastor Jason Carver teaches the importance of embracing your role as a minister of reconciliation. Drawing from 2 Corinthians 5:17-20, you will discover how to extend grace and forgiveness toward your spouse, reflecting God's heart of reconciliation. Pastor Jason emphasizes that repentance begins with you—allowing God to search your heart and reveal areas that need change. This session challenges you to trust God's kindness to lead your spouse to repentance and encourages you to walk in humility, grace, and hope as you partner with God in restoring your marriage.

"If you are a new creation, you have been tasked, you have been called, you have been ordained to be a minister of reconciliation. Never forget that it's God's kindness that leads to repentance. So don't be afraid of showing your spouse kindness. Reject the lie that God's kindness means He approves of their actions." – Jason Carver

Discussion and review from last week's daily readings of "40 Day Stand For Marriage Restoration."

Before you begin this week's teaching video, go around the group and discuss your insights and takeaways from each of the daily readings from last week. Revisit last week's Day 6 Workbook page for an overview of your reading takeaways.

Write any insights from other group members below:

Any specific day from last week's reading that you need to go back and read again?

Before you begin this week's Video Teaching, pray for the Holy Spirit to come and bring revelation to your stand for restoration as you watch this week's teaching.

Follow along with this week's teaching video and fill in the blanks below as the answers appear on the screen.

Session 3 **VIDEO GUIDE** **STANDING FOR MARRIAGE RESTORATION**

1) _____ have been ordained by God to be a _____ of _____ to the people around you!

2) As a minister of reconciliation, you must learn to not count your spouse's _____ against them.

3) Repentance starts with _____!

4) Repentance opens the door for times of _____ to come into your life!

5) Yes, _____ is needed for the restoration of your marriage to occur but most people are _____ of how to _____ partner with God to help others repent.

6) I never want to be on the same side as the _____. I will not pray for things the devil is wanting my spouse to experience!

7) While God's discipline is a reality and can lead to repentance, it is _____ who decides the form and timing of such discipline, _____ us.

8) If you are desiring your spouse to go through hardships, you should probably examine the levels of _____, _____, and _____ that are still present in your heart.

9) Do not be afraid of God showing your spouse _____! Reject the lie that God's kindness means He _____ of their actions.

10) God's _____ is the biblical agent that brings forth repentance!

11) Pray God gives _____ you and your spouse the _____ of being able to repent!

Discussion Questions from This Week's Teaching Video

Question #1: What are your thoughts on the idea that you have been ordained by God to be a minister of reconciliation? Have you always thought this was something only God did, or do you see your role in it?

Question #2: How difficult is it for you right now to not count your spouse's sins against them and to avoid defining them by their worst moments? What steps can you take to see them through God's eyes?

Question #3: How well are you doing with repentance, starting with you and not your spouse? Have you experienced times of refreshing in your life as a result of your repentance?

Question #4: How does Jason's perspective on partnering with God to bring repentance differ from the idea of "praying them into the pigpen"? Which approach do you believe aligns more with the heart of Jesus and the Father? How can **Galatians 6:1 and Romans 2:4 guide us on this topic?**

Question #5: Have you ever found yourself praying for things that actually align more with what the devil would want to happen to your spouse? How can you shift your prayers to align more with God's will and heart for your spouse?

Question #6: While God's discipline is a reality and can lead to repentance, it is God who decides the form and timing of such discipline, not us. How do you handle the desire for God to discipline your spouse, and how can you trust God's timing and methods?

Question #7: If you find yourself wishing hardships on your spouse, what underlying hurt, bitterness, and unforgiveness might still be present in your heart? How can you begin to heal these areas and move toward forgiveness and compassion?

Question #8: Do you ever fear that by God showing your spouse kindness and blessings it means He approves of their actions? How can you reject this thought and trust in God's kindness, leading to repentance?

Question #9: Have you witnessed how kindness actually helps people change their actions? Can you share any experiences where kindness made a difference in your life or someone else's?

Question #10: How might your stand for your marriage look differently if you fully embraced the truth of Romans 4:17 *(God gives life to the dead and calls into existence what does not exist)*? Discuss how Romans 4:17 empowered Abraham in verses 18-21 and consider how this could apply to your own situation.

This Week's Memory Verses

- *2 Corinthians 5:18 (NIV)* "*All this is from God, who reconciled us to himself through Christ and gave us the ministry of reconciliation:*"

- *Romans 4:17b (ESV)* "*…who gives life to the dead and calls into existence the things that do not exist.*"

- *(Bonus memory verses) - Romans 2:4b (NIV)* "*…not realizing that God's kindness leads you toward repentance?*"

This Week's Daily Readings from "40 Day Stand for Marriage Restoration"

- Day 1: "DAY 8 - YOU ARE A MINISTER OF RECONCILIATION!" (Pages 58 - 65)

- Day 2: "DAY 9 - KINDNESS LEADS TO REPENTANCE" (Pages 66 - 73)

- Day 3: "DAY 10 - CALLS INTO EXISTENCE WHAT DOES NOT EXIST" (Pages 74 - 81)

- Day 4: "DAY 27 - THE WOMAN WILL RETURN TO THE MAN" (Pages 200 - 206)

- Day 5: "DAY 38 - A LITTLE SUFFERING, BUT HE WILL RESTORE!" (Pages 286 - 292)

Scriptures From This Week's Video Teaching

2 Corinthians 5:17–20 (NIV) "[17]*Therefore, if anyone is in Christ, he is a new creation; the old has gone, the new has come!* [18]*All this is from God, who reconciled us to himself through Christ and gave us the ministry of reconciliation:* [19]*that God was reconciling the world to himself in Christ, not counting men's sins against them. And he has committed to us the message of reconciliation.* [20]*We are therefore Christ's ambassadors, as though God were making his appeal through us. We implore you on Christ's behalf: Be reconciled to God.*"

Psalm 139:23–24 (NIV) "[23]*Search me, O God, and know my heart; test me and know my anxious thoughts.* [24]*See if there is any offensive way in me, and lead me in the way everlasting.*"

Acts 3:19 (NIV) "*Repent, then, and turn to God, so that your sins may be wiped out, that times of refreshing may come from the Lord.*"

Luke 15:16–24 (NIV) *"¹⁶He longed to fill his stomach with the pods that the pigs were eating, but no one gave him anything. ¹⁷"When he came to his senses, he said, 'How many of my father's hired men have food to spare, and here I am starving to death! ¹⁸I will set out and go back to my father and say to him: Father, I have sinned against heaven and against you. ¹⁹I am no longer worthy to be called your son; make me like one of your hired men.' ²⁰So he got up and went to his father. "But while he was still a long way off, his father saw him and was filled with compassion for him; he ran to his son, threw his arms around him and kissed him. ²¹"The son said to him, 'Father, I have sinned against heaven and against you. I am no longer worthy to be called your son.' ²²"But the father said to his servants, 'Quick! Bring the best robe and put it on him. Put a ring on his finger and sandals on his feet. ²³Bring the fattened calf and kill it. Let's have a feast and celebrate. ²⁴For this son of mine was dead and is alive again; he was lost and is found.' So they began to celebrate."*

Hebrews 12:5-7 (NIV) *"And have you completely forgotten this word of encouragement that addresses you as a father addresses his son? It says, 'My son, do not make light of the Lord's discipline, and do not lose heart when he rebukes you, because the Lord disciplines the one he loves, and he chastens everyone he accepts as his son.' Endure hardship as discipline; God is treating you as his children. For what children are not disciplined by their father?"*

Galatians 6:1 (NIV) *"Brothers and sisters, if someone is caught in a sin, you who live by the Spirit should restore that person gently. But watch yourselves, or you also may be tempted."* ***Romans 2:4b (NIV)*** *"... not realizing that God's kindness leads you toward repentance?"*

Acts 5:31 (NIV) *³¹God exalted him to his own right hand as Prince and Savior that he might give repentance and forgiveness of sins to Israel.*

Acts 11:18 (ESV) *¹⁸When they heard these things they fell silent. And they glorified God, saying, "Then to the Gentiles also God has granted repentance that leads to life."*

2 Timothy 2:24–26 (ESV) *"²⁴And the Lord's servant must not be quarrelsome but kind to everyone, able to teach, patiently enduring evil, ²⁵correcting his opponents with gentleness. God may perhaps grant them repentance leading to a knowledge of the truth, ²⁶and they may come to their senses and escape from the snare of the devil, after being captured by him to do his will."*

Romans 4:17–22 (ESV) *"¹⁷as it is written, "I have made you the father of many nations"—in the presence of the God in whom he believed, who gives life to the dead and calls into existence the things that do not exist. ¹⁸In hope he believed against hope, that he should become the father of many nations, as he had been told, "So shall your offspring be." ¹⁹He did not weaken in faith when he considered his own body, which was as good as dead (since he was about a hundred years old), or when he considered the barrenness of Sarah's womb. ²⁰No unbelief made him waver concerning the promise of God, but he grew strong in his faith as he gave glory to God, ²¹fully convinced that God was able to do what he had promised. ²²That is why his faith was "counted to him as righteousness.""*

SESSION 3 - DAY 1

DAY 8 - YOU ARE A MINISTER OF RECONCILIATION!

2 Corinthians 5:18 (ESV) "All this is from God, who through Christ reconciled us to himself and gave us the ministry of reconciliation;"

Read pages Pages 58 – 65: <u>**Day 8 – You Are a Minister of Reconciliation**</u> from "40 Day Stand For Marriage Restoration."

Stand on this truth:

You are a minister of reconciliation. Let's explore 2 Corinthians 5:18 and reflect on how embracing this truth empowers us in our stand for marriage restoration. In the midst of standing for the restoration of your marriage, remember that you are not merely a bystander but a chosen vessel entrusted with the ministry of reconciliation. God has ordained every believer to carry out this divine assignment.

Prayer for Today:

"Heavenly Father, thank you for entrusting me with the ministry of reconciliation. Help me to embrace this calling with humility and confidence. Grant me the wisdom, strength, and love to carry out this ministry effectively in my marriage. May my actions and words reflect Your transformative power. In Jesus' name, amen."

Activate Today's Lesson:

1. How does embracing your role as a **minister of reconciliation** impact your perspective on marriage restoration?

2. Identify and write down any lies from today's **"Lies to Reject"** that you've been struggling with. Cross them out symbolically to break their hold on your mind.

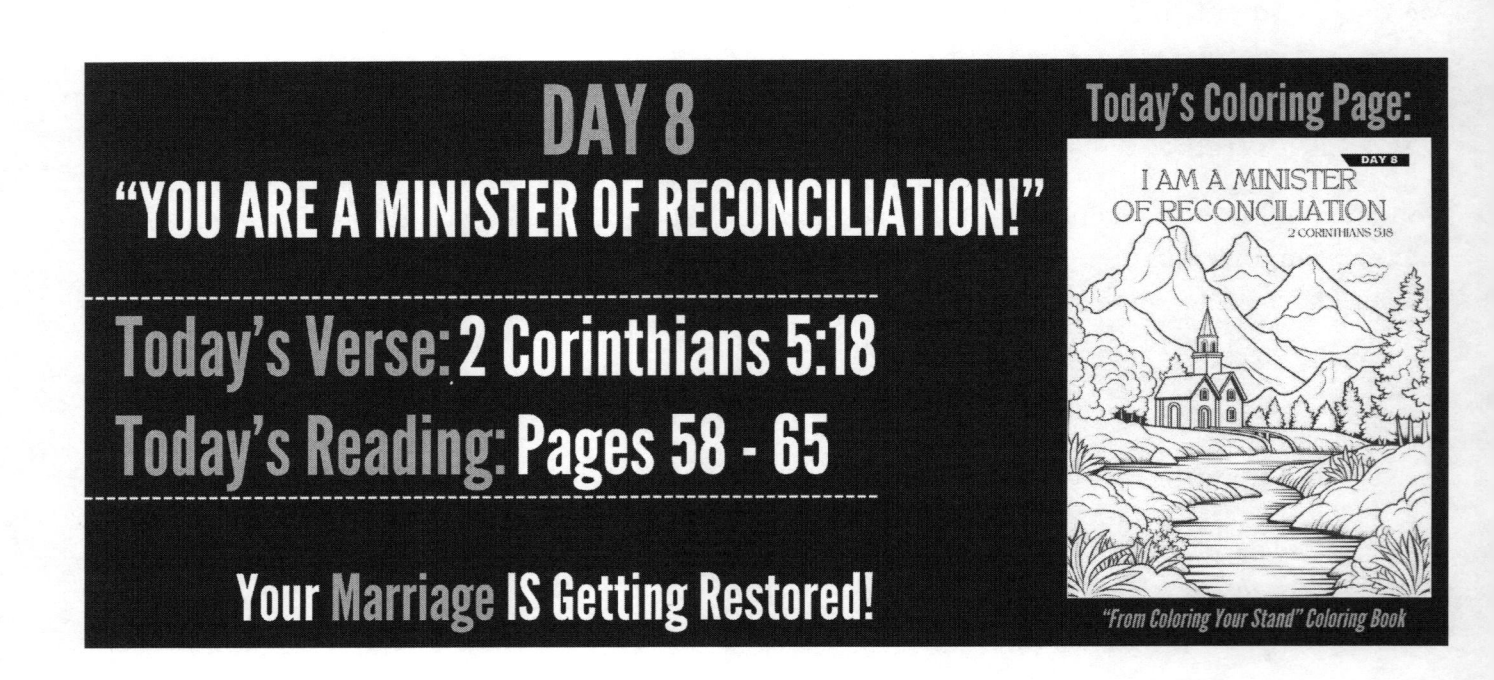

3. Write down below and begin to speak aloud a few of today's **"Daily Truths to Declare."** Believe that they are true and activated in your stand for restoration.

DAY 8
"YOU ARE A MINISTER OF RECONCILIATION!"

Today's Verse: 2 Corinthians 5:18
Today's Reading: Pages 58 - 65

Your Marriage IS Getting Restored!

Today's Coloring Page:
I AM A MINISTER OF RECONCILIATION
2 CORINTHIANS 5:18
"From Coloring Your Stand" Coloring Book

SESSION 3 - DAY 2

DAY 9: KINDNESS LEADS TO REPENTANCE

Romans 2:4 (NASB) "Or do you think lightly of the riches of His kindness and forbearance and patience, not knowing that the kindness of God leads you to repentance?"

Read pages 66 - 73: <u>*Day 9: Kindness Leads to Repentance*</u> from "40 Day Stand For Marriage Restoration."

Stand on this truth:

Kindness leads to repentance. Let's explore Romans 2:4 and understand how embracing kindness can transform hearts and lead to repentance in our marriages. In our stand for marriage restoration, it's crucial to recognize the transformative power of kindness. Rather than wishing ill will or hardships upon our spouses, let's choose to exhibit kindness, knowing that it can soften hearts and lead to repentance.

Prayer for Today:

"Heavenly Father, thank you for the reminder that Your kindness leads to repentance. Help me to extend Your kindness to my spouse, even in difficult times. Grant me the strength to trust Your timing and to believe that Your kindness will soften their heart. May our marriage be restored through Your transformative love. In Jesus' name, amen.

Activate Today's Lesson:

1. How does embracing **kindness** impact your perspective on marriage restoration?

2. Identify and write down any lies from today's **"Lies to Reject"** that you've been struggling with. Cross them out symbolically to break their hold on your mind.

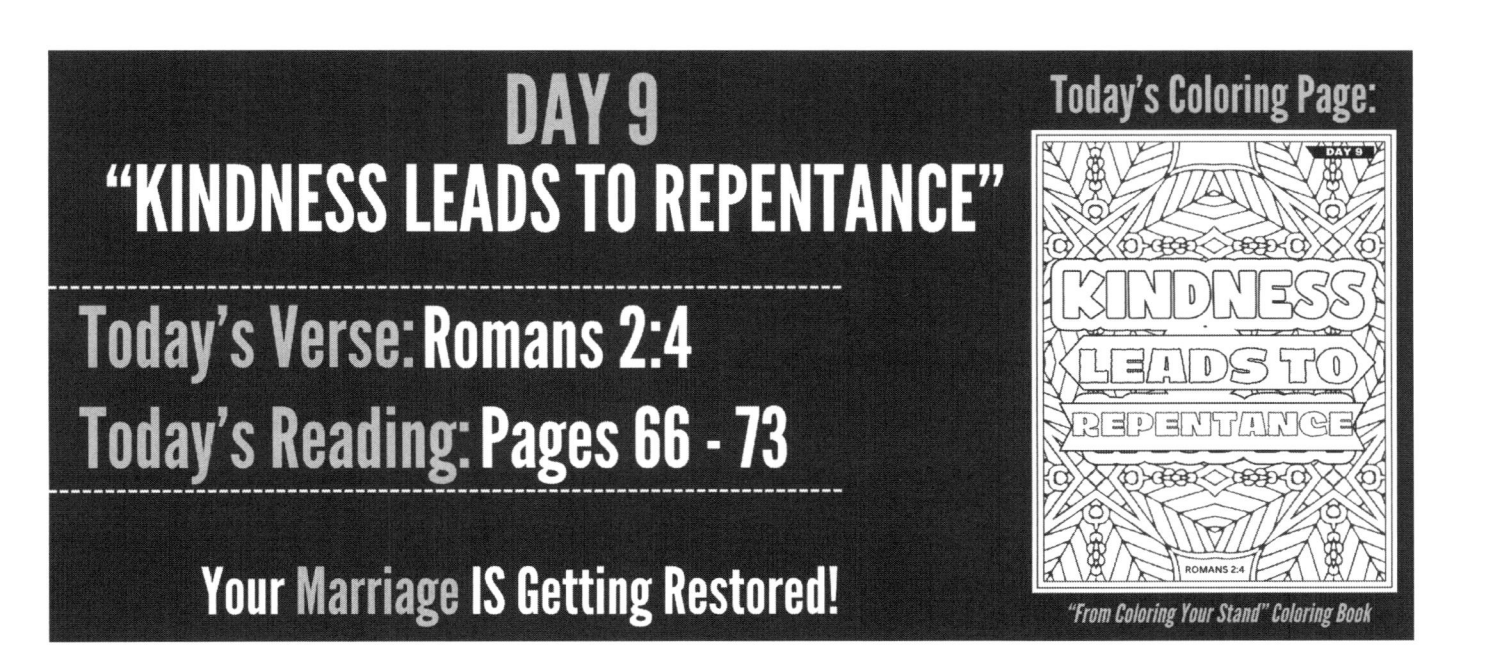

3. Write down below and begin to speak aloud a few of today's **"Daily Truths to Declare."** Believe that they are true and activated in your stand for restoration.

DAY 9
"KINDNESS LEADS TO REPENTANCE"

Today's Verse: **Romans 2:4**
Today's Reading: **Pages 66 - 73**

Your Marriage IS Getting Restored!

Today's Coloring Page:

"From Coloring Your Stand" Coloring Book

SESSION 3 - DAY 3

DAY 10: CALLS INTO EXISTENCE WHAT DOES NOT EXIST

Session 3 - Day 4

Day 27: The Woman Will Return to the Man

Jeremiah 31:22 (NIV) "How long will you wander, unfaithful Daughter Israel? The Lord will create a new thing on earth— the woman will return to the man."

Read pages 200 - 206: <u>*Day 27: The Woman Will Return to the Man*</u> from "40 Day Stand For Marriage Restoration."

Stand on this truth:

In the midst of your spouse's wandering and unfaithfulness, Jeremiah 31:22 offers a beacon of hope and assurance. This verse declares, *"How long will you wander, unfaithful Daughter Israel? The Lord will create a new thing on earth— the woman will return to the man."* Despite the challenges you face, God's plan for restoration remains steadfast. God's promise of restoration transcends the limitations of our circumstances. Regardless of how far your spouse has strayed or how bleak the situation may seem, God is actively working to create something new in your marriage. He specializes in redeeming what seems irreparable, and His plan includes the return of the wandering spouse to their partner.

Prayer for Today:

"Heavenly Father, thank You for the promise of restoration found in Jeremiah 31:22. Despite the challenges and pain, I choose to trust in Your ability to create a new thing in my marriage. I declare that Your promise holds true for me: "The woman will return to the man." Strengthen my faith, Lord, and help me to stand firm in Your perfect plan. In Jesus' name, amen."

Activate Today's Lesson:

1. How does embracing the truth that **"The Woman Will Return to the Man"** impact your stand for marriage restoration?

2. Identify and write down any lies from today's **"Lies to Reject"** that you've been struggling with. Cross them out symbolically to break their hold on your mind.

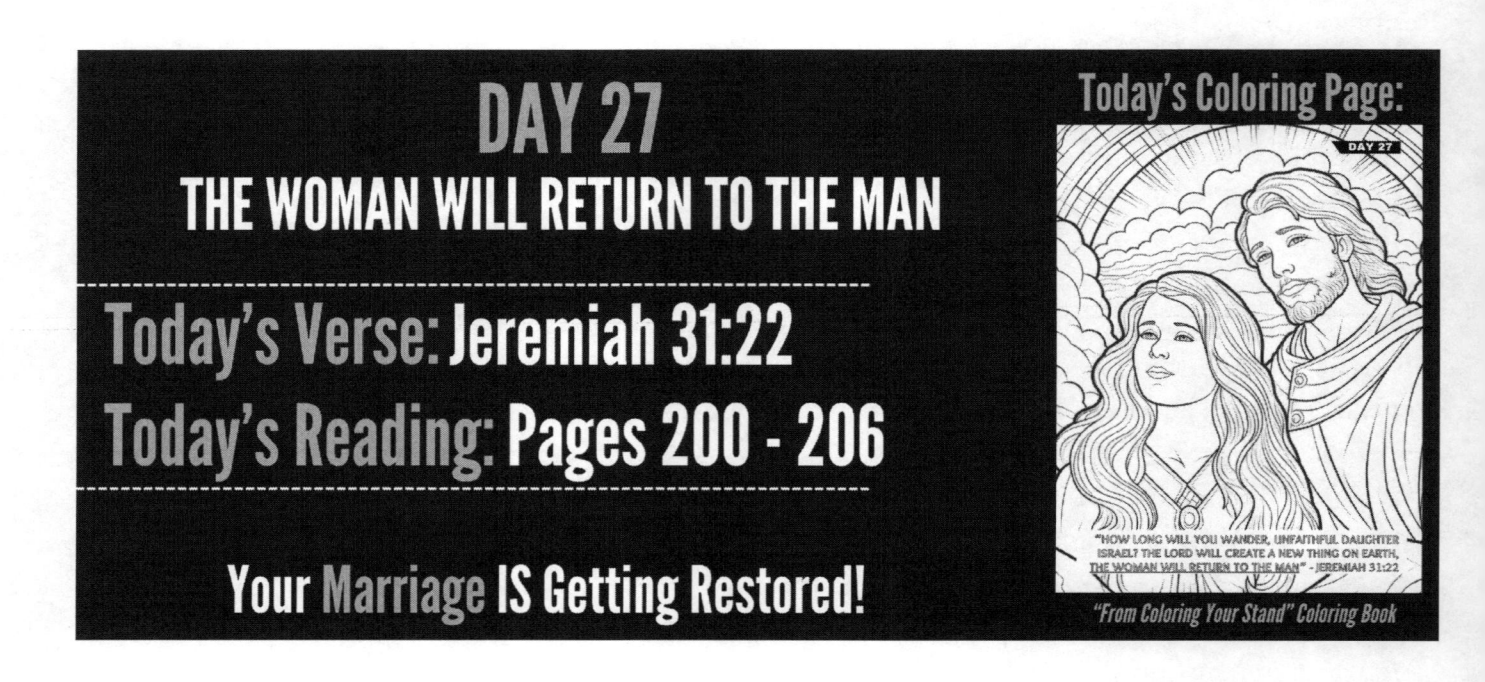

3. Write down below and begin to speak aloud a few of today's **"Daily Truths to Declare."** Believe that they are true and activated in your stand for restoration.

DAY 27
THE WOMAN WILL RETURN TO THE MAN

Today's Verse: Jeremiah 31:22
Today's Reading: Pages 200 - 206

Your Marriage IS Getting Restored!

Today's Coloring Page:

"HOW LONG WILL YOU WANDER, UNFAITHFUL DAUGHTER ISRAEL? THE LORD WILL CREATE A NEW THING ON EARTH, THE WOMAN WILL RETURN TO THE MAN" - JEREMIAH 31:22

"From Coloring Your Stand" Coloring Book

Session 3 - Day 5

Day 38: A Little Suffering, But He Will Restore!

1 Peter 5:10b (NLT) "...So after you have suffered a little while, he will restore, support, and strengthen you, and he will place you on a firm foundation."

Read pages 286 - 292: *Day 38: A Little Suffering, But He Will Restore!* from "40 Day Stand For Marriage Restoration."

Stand on this truth:

Suffering is an inevitable part of life, especially when standing for the restoration of a marriage. However, the suffering we endure is temporary, and it serves a purpose in preparing us for the restoration that God promises. This verse assures us that after a period of suffering, God will restore, support, strengthen, and establish us on a firm foundation.

Prayer for Today:

"Heavenly Father, I come before You with a heart believing for the restoration of my marriage. In moments of suffering, I find peace in Your presence, knowing that You will strengthen and help me. Uphold me with Your righteous right hand, guiding me through this journey. Thank You for the promise of restoration and for setting my feet on a firm foundation. In Jesus' name, amen."

Activate Today's Lesson:

1. Which promise from 1 Peter 5:10b do you need to be reminded of today (restoration, support, strength, or firm foundation)? How does the truth of temporary suffering impact your stand for marriage restoration?

2. Identify and write down any lies from today's **"Lies to Reject"** that you've been struggling with. Cross them out symbolically to break their hold on your mind.

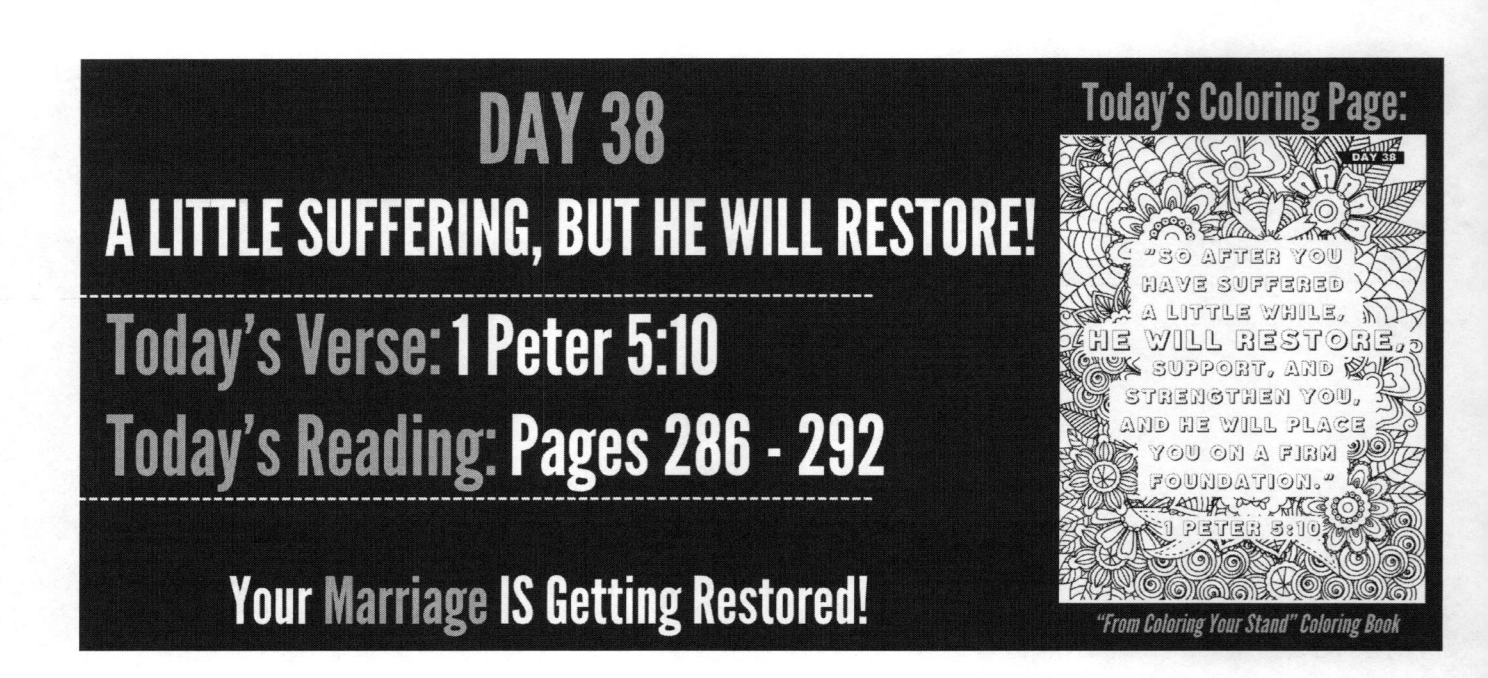

3. Write down below and begin to speak aloud a few of today's **"Daily Truths to Declare."** Believe that they are true and activated in your stand for restoration.

DAY 38

A LITTLE SUFFERING, BUT HE WILL RESTORE!

Today's Verse: **1 Peter 5:10**

Today's Reading: **Pages 286 - 292**

Your Marriage IS Getting Restored!

Today's Coloring Page:

"So after you have suffered a little while, He will restore, support, and strengthen you, and He will place you on a firm foundation."
— 1 Peter 5:10

"From Coloring Your Stand" Coloring Book

SESSION 3 - DAY 6

REVIEWING THIS WEEK'S DAILY READINGS

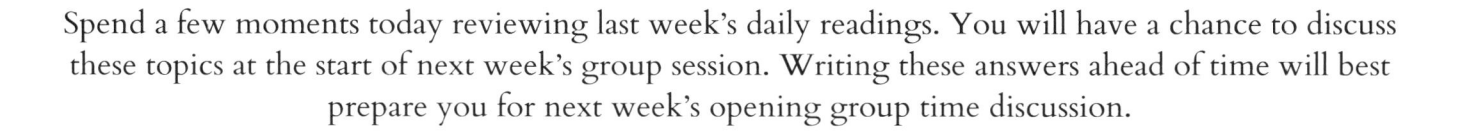

Spend a few moments today reviewing last week's daily readings. You will have a chance to discuss these topics at the start of next week's group session. Writing these answers ahead of time will best prepare you for next week's opening group time discussion.

What encouraging takeaways did you have from this day's reading? What specific thoughts, verses, lies, declarations, or testimonies are specifically impactful for your stand?

Day 1 – "Day 8: You Are a Minister of Reconciliation!" insights:

Day 2 – "Day 9: Kindness Leads to Repentance" insights:

Day 3 – "Day 10: Calls Into Existence What Does Not Exist" insights:

Day 4 – "Day 27: The Woman Will Return to the Man" insights:

Day 5 – "Day 38: A Little Suffering, But He Will Restore!" insights:

Write this week's Memory Verse below:

Additional Notes:

SESSION 4 - STANDING WITH A HEALED HEART: GRIEF, SHAME, FEAR, AND FORGIVENESS

In session 4, "Standing With a Healed Heart," Pastor Jason Carver addresses the importance of emotional healing during your stand for marriage restoration. He explores four key areas that require God's touch: grief, shame, fear, and forgiveness. By allowing God to heal these wounds, you can stand with greater strength, peace, and faith. Pastor Jason reminds you that God's love drives out fear, removes shame, and empowers you to forgive your spouse as you have been forgiven. This session invites you to bring your pain before God, allowing Him to restore your heart and equip you to stand supernaturally.

"Grieving the death of your marriage doesn't mean you lack faith for its resurrection. It just means you're processing your emotions healthily. God blesses those who mourn in His presence." – Jason Carver

Discussion and review from last week's daily readings of "40 Day Stand For Marriage Restoration."

Before you begin this week's teaching video, go around the group and discuss your insights and takeaways from each of the daily readings from last week. Revisit last week's Day 6 Workbook page for an overview of your reading takeaways.

Write any insights from other group members below:

Any specific day from last week's reading that you need to go back and read again?

Before you begin this week's Video Teaching, pray for the Holy Spirit to come and bring revelation to your stand for restoration as you watch this week's teaching.

Follow along with this week's teaching video and fill in the blanks below as the answers appear on the screen.

Session 4 — **VIDEO GUIDE** — **STANDING FOR MARRIAGE RESTORATION**

1) Grieving the death of your marriage doesn't mean you lack _____ for the resurrection; it just means you are processing your emotions _____.

2) God _____ you when you mourn in His presence!

3) Don't ever be _____ for standing for your marriage.

4) The enemy will use _____ to cripple your heart as you stand for restoration.

5) When you sense fear rising in your heart ask God to give you more _____, more _____, and His _____ _____.

6) Every time fear rises in your heart, ask for _____ _____ to come and drive it out!

7) Forgiveness is your part, whether they respond or not, whether they ask for it or not, whether they even recognize they need it or not. You forgive for _____ sake.

8) Begin by praying for the strength to forgive. It may be a _____ process, but it's crucial for your healing and restoration.

Discussion Questions from This Week's Teaching Video

Question #1: What do you think about Jesus weeping over Lazarus even though He was going to resurrect him? How does this show how grieving doesn't mean you lack faith in the miracle?

Question #2: Have you experienced God's presence during an intense time of mourning and grieving? Share how His presence impacted your faith and the healing process.

Question #3: Do you struggle with any of the 15 Lies of Shame and Condemnation Jason mentioned in the video? Read and circle the ones you regularly experience or think about.

1. I must be crazy to think my spouse will ever come back to me.
2. Everyone else seems to have it together; why can't I?
3. I should just give up and move on; it's never going to get better.
4. I must not be praying right or God would have answered by now.
5. I feel like I'm wasting my time by holding onto hope.
6. I'm a failure because I couldn't keep my marriage together.
7. People must think I'm in denial and not facing reality.
8. My spouse is probably happier with someone else.
9. I don't deserve to have my marriage restored after everything that's happened.
10. I should be over this by now; something must be wrong with me.
11. I'm just being foolish to think anything will change.
12. Everyone around me has moved on; why can't I?
13. If my faith were stronger, my marriage would be healed by now.
14. I feel like I'm just making excuses for my spouse's behavior.
15. People probably think I'm pathetic for standing for this marriage.

Question #4: Has the enemy used fear to cripple your heart as you stand for restoration? How could 2 Timothy 1:7 & 1 John 4:18 help when this happens?

Question #5: How do you view forgiveness as your responsibility, regardless of the other person's response or recognition of their need for it? How does forgiving for your own sake impact your healing process?

Question #6: How do you differentiate between forgiveness and trust? What steps do you take to forgive instantly, yet understand that trust must be rebuilt over time through actions?

Question #7: I know it's hard sometimes to forgive. What can we do when it's a struggle? How can asking God for help to forgive, even if it might be a gradual process, contribute to your healing and restoration?

***** BONUS HANDOUT – "Godly Grieving Over Your Marriage ******

We have a **BONUS HANDOUT** for you this week, which includes a special **"Godly Grieving Over Your Marriage"** exercise. This exercise is designed to help you process your emotions in a healthy, faith-filled way.

I encourage each of you to spend some time this week going through the Godly Grieving handout. Use this exercise to invite God into your pain and allow Him to bring healing and comfort to your heart. Remember, acknowledging your grief and emotions is a vital part of the healing process and can strengthen your faith as you stand for your marriage. Take this opportunity to reflect, pray, and let God's presence minister to you in a deep way this week.

This Week's Memory Verses

- Each week, we will have a memory verse to help us focus on God's promises and build our faith. These verses are designed to encourage and strengthen us as we stand for the restoration of our marriages. Let's take a moment to reflect on this week's verse and allow it to resonate in our hearts throughout the week.

Matthew 5:4 (NIV) "Blessed are those who mourn, for they shall be comforted."

(Bonus memory verses) - *1 John 4:18 (NIV)* "There is no fear in love. But perfect love drives out fear, because fear has to do with punishment. The one who fears is not made perfect in love."

This Week's Daily Readings from "40 Day Stand for Marriage Restoration"

- *Day 1:* "DAY 35: IT'S OK TO GRIEVE, JESUS DID" (Pages 262 - 269)

- *Day 2:* "DAY 18 - NO MORE SHAME" (Pages 134 - 141)

- *Day 3:* "DAY 28 - FEAR IS NOT YOUR FRIEND" (Pages 207 - 214)

- *Day 4:* "DAY 17 - WAITING QUIETLY" (Pages 127 - 133)

- *Day 5:* "DAY 13 - LOVE CONQUERS THE CALENDAR" (Pages 98 - 105)

- *Day 6:* "Reviewing This Week's Daily Readings" (Workbook)

Scriptures From This Week's Video Teaching

John 11:35 (ESV) "Jesus wept."

Psalm 62:8 (ESV) "Trust in him at all times, O people; pour out your heart before him; God is a refuge for us."

1 Peter 5:7 (NIV) "Cast all your anxiety on him because he cares for you."

Psalm 34:19 (ESV) "Many are the afflictions of the righteous, but the LORD delivers him out of them all."

Matthew 5:4 (NIV) "Blessed are those who mourn, for they shall be comforted.

Psalm 25:3a (NIV) "No one who hopes in you will ever be put to shame..."

Romans 8:1 (ESV) "There is therefore now no condemnation for those who are in Christ Jesus."

Psalm 56:3–4 (NIV) "³When I am afraid, I will trust in you. ⁴In God, whose word I praise, in God I trust; I will not be afraid. What can mortal man do to me?"

2 Timothy 1:7 (NKJV) "For God has not given us a spirit of fear, but of power and of love and of a sound mind."

1 John 4:18 (NIV) "There is no fear in love. But perfect love drives out fear, because fear has to do with punishment. The one who fears is not made perfect in love."

Isaiah 41:10 (NIV) "So do not fear, for I am with you; do not be dismayed, for I am your God. I will strengthen you and help you; I will uphold you with my righteous right hand."

Matthew 18:21–23 (NIV) ²¹Then Peter came to Jesus and asked, "Lord, how many times shall I forgive my brother when he sins against me? Up to seven times?" ²²Jesus answered, "I tell you, not seven times, but seventy-seven times. ²³"Therefore, the kingdom of heaven is like a king who wanted to settle accounts with his servants.

Colossians 3:13 (NIV) "Bear with each other and forgive one another if any of you has a grievance against someone. Forgive as the Lord forgave you."

2 Corinthians 5:18–19 (NIV) "¹⁸All this is from God, who reconciled us to himself through Christ and gave us the ministry of reconciliation: ¹⁹that God was reconciling the world to himself in Christ, not counting men's sins against them. And he has committed to us the message of reconciliation."

Luke 7:47 (NKJV) "Therefore I say to you, her sins, which are many, are forgiven, for she loved much. But to whom little is forgiven, the same loves little."

Godly Grieving Over Your Marriage Activation Handouts

Use this **BONUS HANDOUT** to help you process your grief. This special **"Godly Grieving Over Your Marriage"** activation assignment is designed to help you process the emotions of your marriage situation in a healthy, faith-filled way.

I encourage each of you to spend some time this week going through the **"Godly Grieving Over Your Marriage"** handout. Use this exercise to invite God into your pain and allow Him to bring healing and comfort to your heart. Remember, acknowledging your grief and emotions is a vital part of the healing process and can strengthen your faith as you stand for your marriage. Take this opportunity to reflect, pray, and let God's presence minister to you in a deep way this week.

The handouts are on the following pages….

Godly Grieving Over Your Marriage
(Adapted From Nothing Hidden Ministries)

Grieving is a natural and necessary part of standing for the restoration of your marriage. The process of Godly grieving allows you to bring your pain to God, receive His comfort, and find healing in His presence. This guide will walk you through the steps of Godly grieving, specifically for those standing for their marriage.

Matthew 5:4 – *"Blessed are those who mourn, for they shall be comforted."*

1. **Acknowledge Your Current Pain**
    Fully acknowledge the pain and suffering you are experiencing in your marriage. Don't try to minimize it or make it go away quickly. Accept that grieving is a necessary step in the healing process.

    Pray: "Father, I give You permission to teach me Godly grieving and take me through this grieving process. Thank You that as I mourn the brokenness in my marriage, I will be blessed and comforted."

2. **Communicate Your Suffering to the Lord**
    Psalm 62:8 – *"Trust in him at all times, O people; pour out your heart before him; God is a refuge for us."*

    Freely communicate your suffering to the Lord. He is your refuge and safe place. Express your feelings openly and honestly to God.

    Activity #1: *Write a letter to God describing your emotions, fears, and struggles related to your marriage. Be as detailed and candid as possible. This is your time to give God your hurts and fears.*

3. **Know that He cares deeply about your tears and sorrows.**
    Revelation 21:4 – *"He will wipe away every tear from their eyes, and death shall be no more, neither shall there be mourning, nor crying, nor pain anymore, for the former things have passed away."*

    Activity #2: Write down the ways you've tried to deal with your pain on your own.

4. **Continue talking to the Lord about your pain and seeking His help.**
    1 Peter 5:7 – *"Cast all your anxiety on him because he cares for you."*

    Activity #3: Write a letter from God to you and let Him speak to you about how He wants to take you through this process. Don't overthink or doubt, just start writing as if God is speaking to you.

5. **When God speaks, obey! You must be willing to follow however He directs you.**
    Psalm 34:19 – *"Many are the afflictions of the righteous, but the LORD delivers him out of them all."*

    Now follow through with the steps God placed on your heart, whether it's seeking counsel, making amends, taking steps towards forgiveness, or just patiently enduring the current hardship.

Conclusion: Grieving is not a sign of weakness but a step towards healing and restoration. By bringing your pain to God, you allow Him to work in your heart and guide you towards a place of peace & healing. Embrace Godly grieving while standing for your marriage and watch new strength and faith arise within you! Be persistent in the healing of your grief. Repeat this process often and as necessary, especially when other issues that need grieving come up. Don't forget, Jesus wept, so make sure you do too!

Need more resources on standing with a healed heart? Our Academy has a multi-week section of videos and activities on this topic. Get more info at: www.StandingSupernaturally.com/Academy

Godly Grieving Over Your Marriage

Activity #1: *Write a letter to God describing your emotions, fears, and struggles related to your marriage. Be as detailed and candid as possible. This is your time to give God your hurts and fears.*

Activity #2: *Write down the ways you've tried to deal with your pain on your own.*

Godly Grieving Over Your Marriage

Activity #3: Write a letter from God to you and let Him speak to you about how He wants to take you through this process. Don't overthink or doubt, just start writing as if God is speaking to you.

Session 4 - Day 1

Day 35: It's Ok to Grieve, Jesus Did!

John 11:35 (ESV) "Jesus wept."

Read pages 262 - 269: **Day 35: It's Ok to Grieve, Jesus Did!** from "40 Day Stand For Marriage Restoration."

Stand on this truth:

In John 11:35, we read the shortest verse in the Bible: "Jesus wept." This powerful moment teaches us that even Jesus, the Son of God, allowed Himself to grieve. As we stand for the restoration of our marriages, it's crucial to understand that it's okay to acknowledge and process our emotions, including grief. Grieving the loss of a marriage doesn't diminish our faith; it's a natural and healthy response to pain and brokenness. Just as Jesus grieved at the tomb of Lazarus, we can bring our sorrow to God, trusting Him to comfort us and bring healing to our hearts.

Prayer for Today:

"Heavenly Father, thank you for the example of Jesus, who showed us that it's okay to grieve. Help me to embrace my emotions and bring them to You for healing. Comfort me in my sorrow, knowing that You are close to the brokenhearted. May Your love and grace sustain me as I stand for the restoration of my marriage. Amen."

Activate Today's Lesson:

1. How does embracing the truth that it's **ok to grieve** impact your stand for marriage restoration?

2. Identify and write down any lies from today's **"Lies to Reject"** that you've been struggling with. Cross them out symbolically to break their hold on your mind.

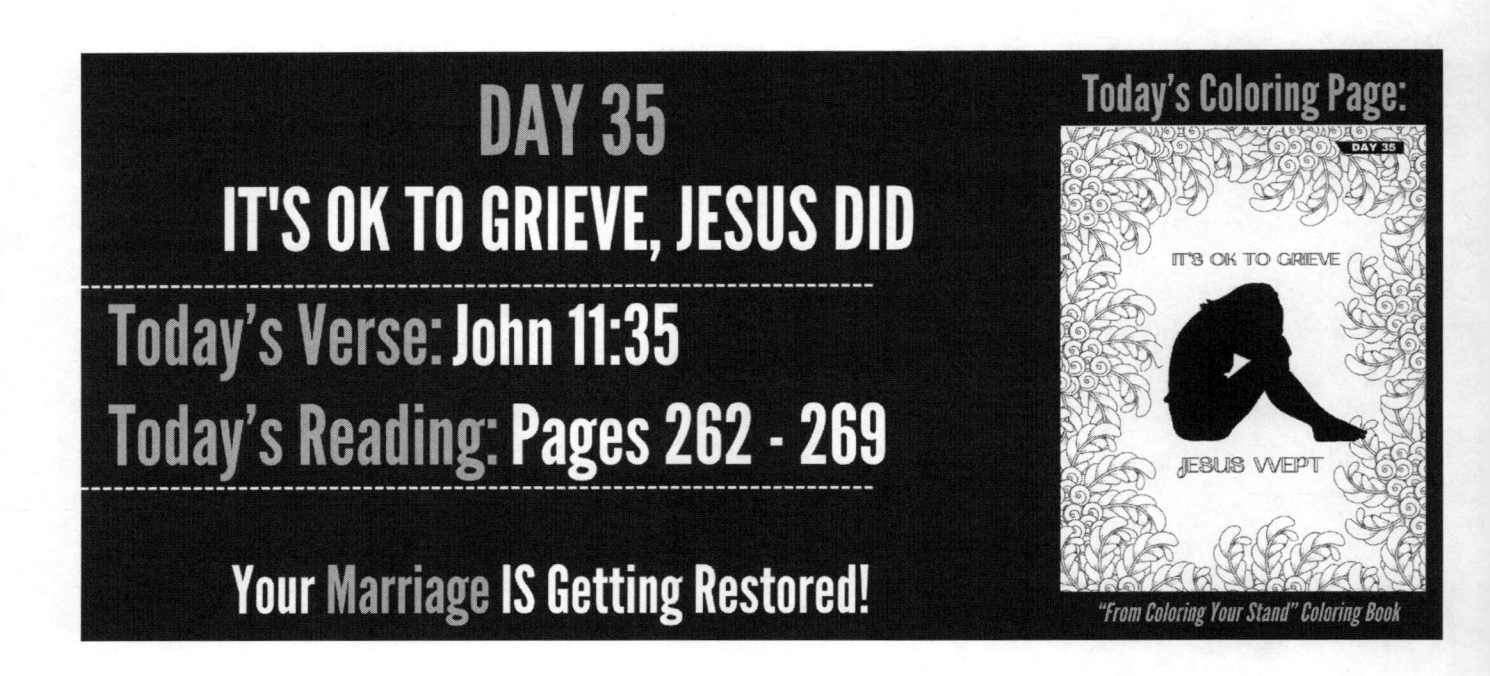

3. Write down below and begin to speak aloud a few of today's **"Daily Truths to Declare."** Believe that they are true and activated in your stand for restoration.

DAY 35
IT'S OK TO GRIEVE, JESUS DID

Today's Verse: John 11:35
Today's Reading: Pages 262 - 269

Your Marriage IS Getting Restored!

Today's Coloring Page:

IT'S OK TO GRIEVE
JESUS WEPT

"From Coloring Your Stand" Coloring Book

Session 4 - Day 2

Day 18: No More Shame

Psalm 25:3a (NIV) "No one who hopes in you will ever be put to shame..."

Read pages 134 - 141: **Day 18: No More Shame** from "40 Day Stand For Marriage Restoration."

Stand on this truth:

In the face of doubt and skepticism from others, it's essential to remember that those who hope in the Lord will never be put to shame (Psalm 25:3a). Are you feeling the disapproval and skepticism of others as you stand for your marriage? Do you find yourself almost ashamed of your commitment to restoration? Remember, Psalm 25:3a assures us that those who place their hope in the Lord will never be put to shame.

Prayer for Today:

"Heavenly Father, I choose to place my hope in You, knowing that You are faithful and powerful to bring restoration. Strengthen my faith, Lord, and remove any shame that the enemy tries to throw at me. Thank You for Your unfailing love and the promise of restoration. In Jesus' name, amen.".

Activate Today's Lesson:

1. Have you experienced ridicule or negativity because of your stand for your marriage? How can embracing the truth of **NO MORE SHAME** impact your journey?

2. Identify and write down any lies from today's **"Lies to Reject"** that you've been struggling with. Cross them out symbolically to break their hold on your mind.

3. Write down below and begin to speak aloud a few of today's **"Daily Truths to Declare."** Believe that they are true and activated in your stand for restoration.

DAY 18
NO MORE SHAME

Today's Verse: **Psalm 25:3**
Today's Reading: **Pages 134 - 141**

Your Marriage IS Getting Restored!

Today's Coloring Page:

NO ONE WHO HOPES IN YOU WILL EVER BE PUT TO SHAME.
PSALM 25:3

"From Coloring Your Stand" Coloring Book

Session 4 - Day 3

Day 28: Fear Is Not Your Friend!

2 Timothy 1:7 (NKJV) "For God has not given us a spirit of fear, but of power and of love and of a sound mind."

Read pages 207 - 214: **Day 28: Fear Is Not Your Friend!** from "40 Day Stand For Marriage Restoration."

Stand on this truth:

In the face of uncertainty and doubt, it's common for fear to grip our hearts and minds, threatening to derail our stand for marriage restoration. However, as believers, we have been equipped with divine resources to combat fear and stand firm in faith. Fear is a weapon the enemy often uses to hinder our faith and undermine our confidence in God's promises. However, 2 Timothy 1:7 reassures us that fear does not originate from God. Instead, He has endowed us with three powerful gifts: power, love, and a sound mind to overcome fear's grip.

Prayer for Today:

"Heavenly Father, I thank You for the promise of power, love, and a sound mind as I stand for the restoration of my marriage. Help me to renounce fear and embrace Your divine gifts, knowing that Your hand is at work in my life. Strengthen me with Your power, fill me with Your love, and guide me with Your sound mind. In Jesus' name, I pray. Amen."

Activate Today's Lesson:

1. How does embracing the truth that **Fear Is Not Your Friend** impact your stand for marriage restoration?

2. Identify and write down any lies from today's **"Lies to Reject"** that you've been struggling with. Cross them out symbolically to break their hold on your mind.

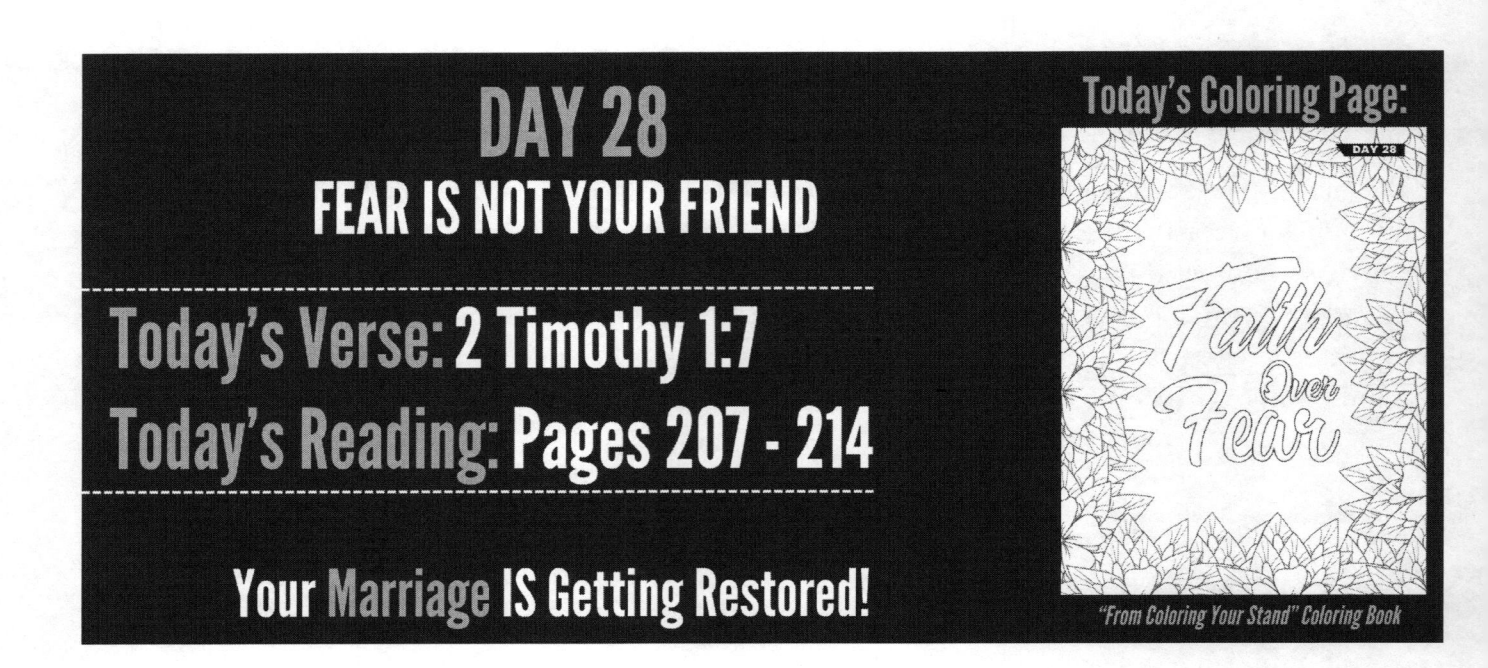

3. Write down below and begin to speak aloud a few of today's **"Daily Truths to Declare."** Believe that they are true and activated in your stand for restoration.

DAY 28
FEAR IS NOT YOUR FRIEND

Today's Verse: **2 Timothy 1:7**
Today's Reading: **Pages 207 - 214**

Your Marriage IS Getting Restored!

Today's Coloring Page:
"From Coloring Your Stand" Coloring Book

Session 4 - Day 4

Day 17: Waiting Quietly

Lamentations 3:25-26 (NIV) "The LORD is good to those whose hope is in him, to the one who seeks him; it is good to wait quietly for the salvation of the LORD."

Read pages 127 – 133: **Day 17: Waiting Quietly** from "40 Day Stand For Marriage Restoration."

Stand on this truth:

In the midst of waiting for the restoration of our marriages, it's crucial to find solace in quietness and trust in God's goodness. In Lamentations 3:25-26, we're reminded of the goodness of the Lord for those who place their hope in Him. Waiting quietly doesn't mean silence but rather finding peace and confidence in God's promises.

Prayer for Today:

"Heavenly Father, teach me to find solace and peace in the quietness of my spirit as I wait for the restoration of my marriage. Help me to trust Your goodness and provision, knowing that Your plans for me are for my ultimate good. Quiet my anxious thoughts, Lord, and fill me with steadfast trust in Your unfailing love. Grant me the patience to wait upon You, confident that Your timing is perfect. In this stillness, I place my hope solely in You, knowing You are faithful to bring beauty from the ashes. In Jesus' name, amen."

Activate Today's Lesson:

1. Reflect on your willingness to wait quietly for the restoration of your marriage. How can embracing the truth of **waiting quietly** impact your stand?

2. Identify and write down any lies from today's **"Lies to Reject"** that you've been struggling with. Cross them out symbolically to break their hold on your mind.

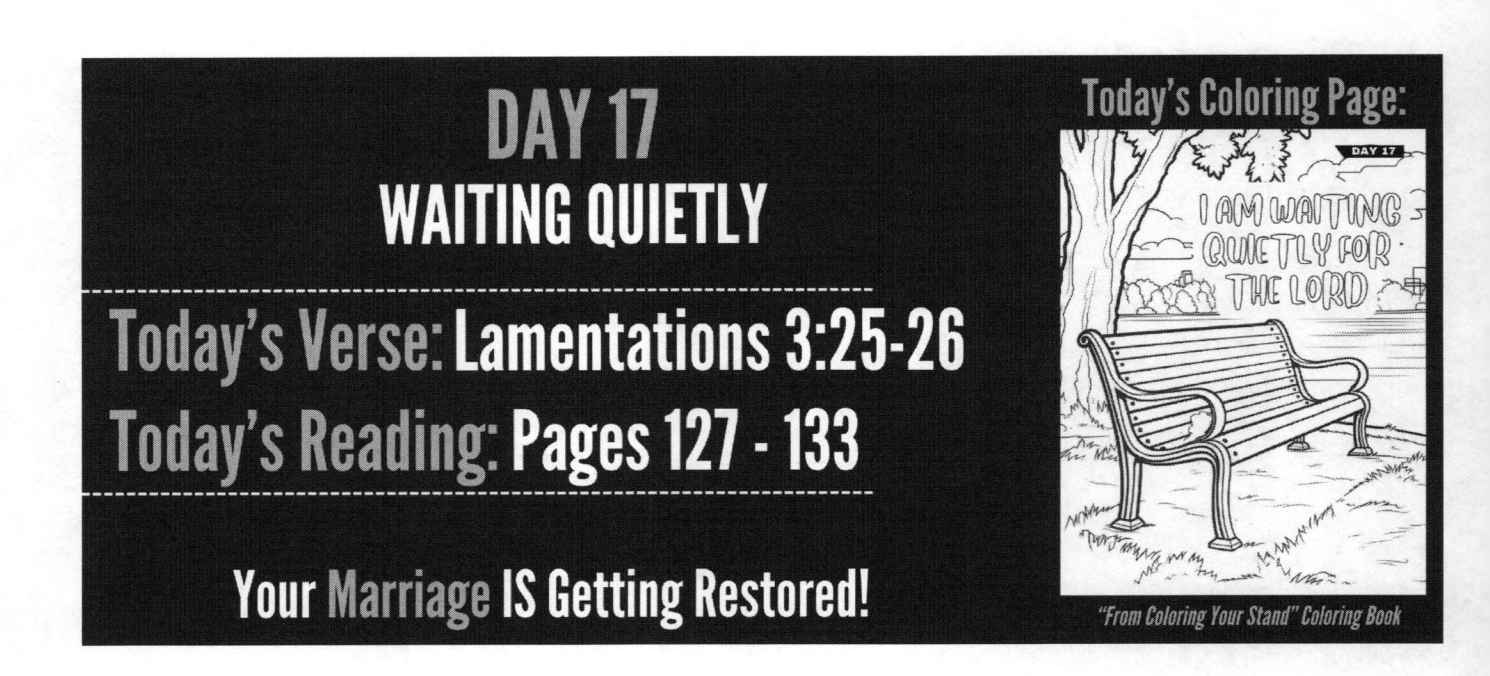

3. Write down below and begin to speak aloud a few of today's **"Daily Truths to Declare."** Believe that they are true and activated in your stand for restoration.

DAY 17
WAITING QUIETLY

Today's Verse: Lamentations 3:25-26
Today's Reading: Pages 127 - 133

Your Marriage IS Getting Restored!

Today's Coloring Page:
I AM WAITING QUIETLY FOR THE LORD
"From Coloring Your Stand" Coloring Book

Session 4 - Day 5

Day 13: Love Conquers the Calendar

Genesis 29:20 (NIV) "So Jacob served seven years to get Rachel, but they seemed like only a few days to him because of his love for her."

Read pages 98 – 105: <u>**Day 13: Love Conquers the Calendar**</u> from "40 Day Stand For Marriage Restoration."

Stand on this truth:

Let's draw inspiration from Genesis 29:20 and understand how love can sustain us through the waiting season of marriage restoration. Time can be one of the most challenging aspects of standing for marriage restoration. But just as Jacob's love for Rachel made seven years feel like mere days, our love for our spouses can conquer the discouraging calendar of time.

Prayer for Today:

"Heavenly Father, just as Jacob's love for Rachel made time seem insignificant, I pray that my love for my spouse will continue to grow stronger each day. Grant me the grace to endure and believe, even in the face of discouragement. Help me reject the lies of the enemy and trust in Your perfect timing. May my unwavering love be a testament to Your faithfulness. In Your loving name, amen."

Activate Today's Lesson:

1. Reflect on how the truth of <u>Genesis 29:20</u> impacts your perspective on waiting for marriage restoration.

2. Identify and write down any lies from today's **"Lies to Reject"** that you've been struggling with. Cross them out symbolically to break their hold on your mind.

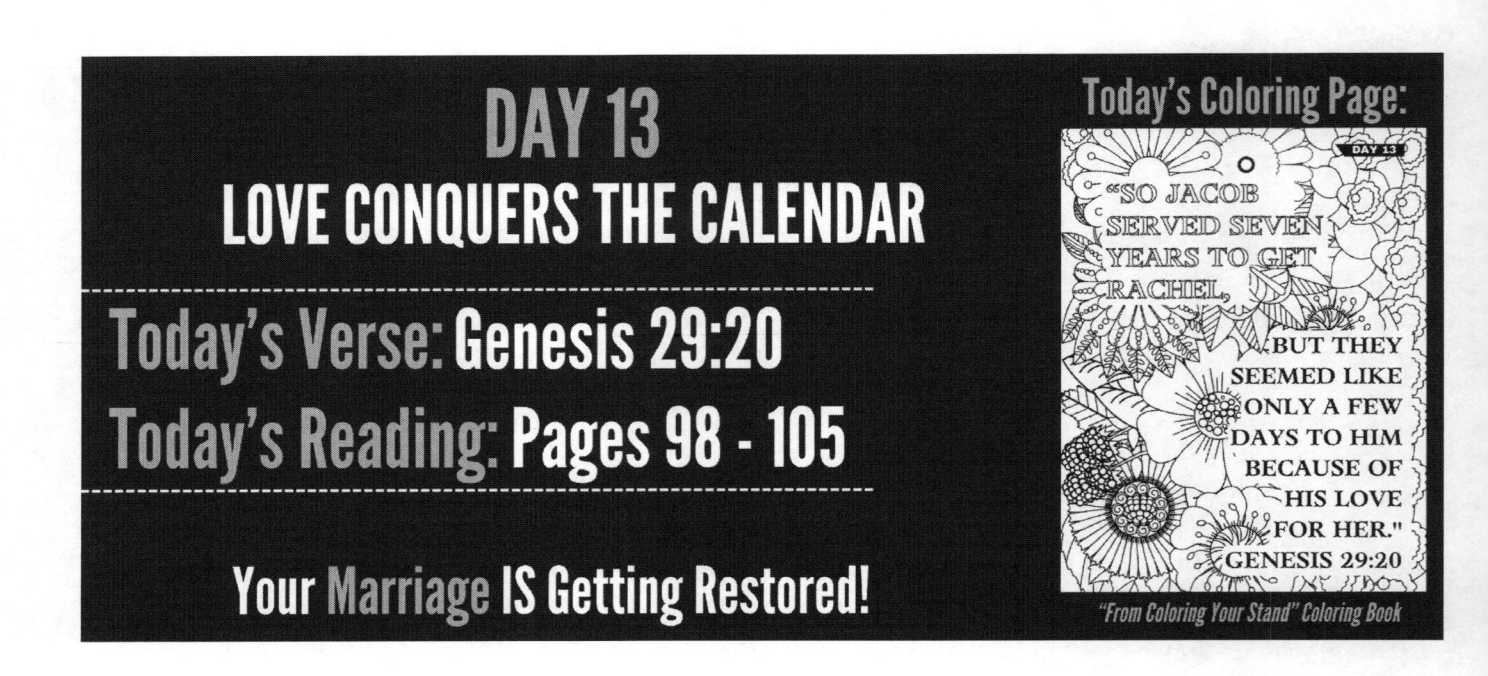

3. Write down below and begin to speak aloud a few of today's **"Daily Truths to Declare."** Believe that they are true and activated in your stand for restoration.

DAY 13

LOVE CONQUERS THE CALENDAR

Today's Verse: Genesis 29:20

Today's Reading: Pages 98 - 105

Your Marriage IS Getting Restored!

Today's Coloring Page:

"SO JACOB SERVED SEVEN YEARS TO GET RACHEL, BUT THEY SEEMED LIKE ONLY A FEW DAYS TO HIM BECAUSE OF HIS LOVE FOR HER." GENESIS 29:20

"From Coloring Your Stand" Coloring Book

Session 4 - Day 6

Reviewing this week's daily readings

Spend a few moments today reviewing last week's daily readings. You will have a chance to discuss these topics at the start of next week's group session. Writing these answers ahead of time will best prepare you for next week's opening group time discussion.

What encouraging takeaways did you have from this day's reading? What specific thoughts, verses, lies, declarations, or testimonies are specifically impactful for your stand?

Day 1 – "Day 35: It's Ok to Grieve, Jesus Did!" insights:

Day 2 – "Day 18: No More Shame" insights:

Day 3 – "Day 28: Fear is Not Your Friend" insights:

Day 4 – "Day 17: Waiting Quietly" insights:

Day 5 – "Day 13: Love Conquers the Calendar" insights:

Write this week's Memory Verse below:

Additional Notes:

Session 5 - The Promise, Price, and Power of Hope

In session 5, "The Promise, Price, and Power of Hope," Pastor Jason Carver shares how hope is a vital anchor during the journey of marriage restoration. You will learn that hope is not wishful thinking but confident expectation in God's promises. Pastor Jason explains the enemy's attempts to steal hope, encouraging you to resist despair and trust that God is working, even in the waiting. By embracing the power of hope, you will find strength, joy, and perseverance to stand firm, knowing that hope in God never puts us to shame.

"Hope changes everything. The enemy's primary attack against your marriage is to steal your hope, but when you cling to God's promises, joy and peace will sustain you through any trial." – Jason Carver

Discussion and review from last week's daily readings of "40 Day Stand For Marriage Restoration."

Before you begin this week's teaching video, go around the group and discuss your insights and takeaways from each of the daily readings from last week. Revisit last week's Day 6 Workbook page for an overview of your reading takeaways.

Write any insights from other group members below:

Any specific day from last week's reading that you need to go back and read again?

Before you begin this week's Video Teaching, pray for the Holy Spirit to come and bring revelation to your stand for restoration as you watch this week's teaching.

Follow along with this week's teaching video and fill in the blanks below as the answers appear on the screen.

Session 5 — VIDEO GUIDE
STANDING FOR MARRIAGE RESTORATION

1) "_____ hope is a _____ _____ and trust in God's promises while providing strength and _____ during trials, that fill us with _____ and peace through the Holy Spirit."

2) The Spiritual battle coming against you is an attack on your _____.

3) There is a sustaining element in having _____ attached to hope.

4) God promises that you will experience His _____ when your hope is truly in Him.

5) Hope always has an element of _____.

6) Hope-filled faith is tested in the _____.

7) Some things will only be won through _____ and _____-_____

8) **THE STOCKDALE PARADOX:** "You must never confuse faith that you will _____ in the end—which you can never afford to lose—with the discipline to confront the most brutal facts of your _____ reality, whatever they might be." - *Admiral Jim Stockdale*

9) "Hope was the most _____ thing I had when standing for my marriage. Hope was the _____ that kept me going when everything else seemed lost." - *Jason Carver*

10) "Hope is being able to **SEE** that there is light **DESPITE** all of the darkness."
   - *Quote from Desmond Tutu*

Discussion Questions from This Week's Teaching Video

Question #1: Pastor Jason mentioned that the spiritual battle coming against you is an attack on your hope. In what ways have you felt your hope being attacked? **How can you stay resilient and hopeful in these spiritual battles?**

Question #2: How could experiencing joy in the midst of trials help sustain your hope? Can you describe a moment when joy and hope together gave you strength?

Question #3: Lamentations 3:25 states, *"The Lord is good to those whose hope is in him."* What are some ways you have experienced God's goodness during your stand?

Question #4: Pastor Jason mentioned that some things will only be won through endurance and long-suffering. Why do you think enduring difficult seasons is essential for victory? How have you seen endurance and long-suffering play out in your own journey of faith?

Question #5: How does the Stockdale Paradox relate to your stand for restoration? *"You must never confuse faith that you will prevail in the end with the discipline to confront the most brutal facts of your current reality."* How can you embrace BOTH of these paradoxical aspects of standing for your marriage? *(Example: You believed restoration would have happened before a specific date; it did not, but you remain steadfast in believing restoration will still come.)*

Question 6: Pray Romans 15:13 together out loud as a group: *"May the God of hope fill me with all joy and peace as I trust in him, so that I may overflow with hope by the power of the Holy Spirit."*

This Week's Memory Verse

- **Psalm 71:14** *(NIV) "As for me, I will always have hope; I will praise you more and more"*
- **(Bonus memory verses)** – **Romans 15:13 (NIV)** *"May the God of hope fill you with all joy and peace as you trust in him, so that you may overflow with hope by the power of the Holy Spirit."*

This Week's Daily Readings from "40 Day Stand for Marriage Restoration"

- *Day 1:* **"DAY 14: THE THREE ELEMENTS OF BREAKTHROUGH"** (Pages 106 – 112)
- *Day 2:* **"DAY 15 – THE PROCESS OF HOPE!"** (Pages 113 – 119)
- *Day 3:* **"DAY 16 – THE PRICE FOR HOPE!"** (Pages 120 – 126)
- *Day 4:* **"DAY 19 – ALWAYS HAVE HOPE"** (Pages 142 – 148)
- *Day 5:* **"DAY 25 – IT WILL BE GREATER THAN BEFORE"** (Pages 186 – 192)
- *Day 6:* "Reviewing This Week's Daily Readings" (Workbook)

Scriptures From This Week's Video Teaching

Hebrews 11:1 (ESV) *"Now faith is the assurance of things hoped for, the conviction of things not seen."*

Matthew 17:20 (NIV) "He replied, "Because you have so little faith. I tell you the truth, if you have faith as small as a mustard seed, you can say to this mountain, 'Move from here to there' and it will move. Nothing will be impossible for you."

Romans 12:6 (NKJV) "Having then gifts differing according to the grace that is given to us, let us use them: if prophecy, let us prophesy in proportion to our faith;"

Hebrews 11:1 (AMP) "NOW FAITH is the assurance (the confirmation, the title deed) of the things [we] hope for, being the proof of things [we] do not see and the conviction of their reality [faith perceiving as real fact what is not revealed to the senses]."

Romans 12:12 (NIV) "Be joyful in hope, patient in affliction, faithful in prayer."

Psalm 51:12 (ESV) "Restore to me the joy of your salvation, and uphold me with a willing spirit."

Nehemiah 8:10b (ESV) "… And do not be grieved, for the joy of the LORD is your strength."

Lamentations 3:25-26 "The LORD is good to those whose hope is in him, to the one who seeks him; it is good to wait quietly for the salvation of the LORD."

Psalm 25:3 (NIV) "No one who hopes in you will ever be put to shame…"

Romans 15:13 (NIV) "May the God of hope fill you with all joy and peace as you trust in him, so that you may overflow with hope by the power of the Holy Spirit."

Romans 8:24–25 (NIV) "[24]For in this hope we were saved. But hope that is seen is no hope at all. Who hopes for what he already has? [25]But if we hope for what we do not yet have, we wait for it patiently."

Romans 5:3-5 (NIV) "Not only so, but we also glory in our sufferings, because we know that suffering produces perseverance; perseverance, character; and character, hope. And hope does not put us to shame, because God's love has been poured out into our hearts through the Holy Spirit, who has been given to us."

James 1:2-4, 12 (NLT) "[2]Dear brothers and sisters, when troubles come your way, consider it an opportunity for great joy. [3]For you know that when your faith is tested, your endurance has a chance to grow. [4]So let it grow, for when your endurance is fully developed, you will be perfect and complete, needing nothing. [12]God blesses those who patiently endure testing and temptation. Afterward they will receive the crown of life that God has promised to those who love him."

Colossians 1:11 (NKJV) "strengthened with all might, according to His glorious power, for all patience and longsuffering with joy;"

Galatians 6:9 (NIV) "Let us not become weary in doing good, for at the proper time we will reap a harvest if we do not give up."

Psalm 71:14 "As for me, I will always have hope; I will praise you more and more."

Haggai 2:9 (KJV) "The glory of this latter house shall be greater than of the former, saith the Lord of hosts: And in this place will I give peace, saith the Lord of hosts."

Session 5 - Day 1

Day 14: The Three Elements of Breakthrough

Romans 12:12 (NIV) "Be joyful in hope, patient in affliction, faithful in prayer."

Read pages 106 – 112: <u>DAY 14: THE THREE ELEMENTS OF BREAKTHROUGH</u> from "40 Day Stand For Marriage Restoration."

Stand on this truth:

In Romans 12:12, we find three powerful elements that pave the way for breakthrough in our stands for marriage restoration. Joy in Hope: Let God's joy fill your heart as you stand in hope for your marriage. Despite the challenges, choose joy as you trust in God's ability to renew and restore. Patience in Affliction: Enduring patiently through difficulties is key to victory. Remember, patience is a fruit of the Holy Spirit, empowering you to outlast the enemy's attacks. Faithfulness in Prayer: Consistent and persistent prayer is essential for breakthrough.

Prayer for Today:

"Heavenly Father, I come before You with a heart filled with hope and trust. I choose to rejoice in the hope of restoration, knowing that You are able to renew and transform my marriage according to Your perfect plan. Grant me patience as I navigate the challenges and difficulties, trusting in Your steadfast love. Help me remain faithful in prayer, seeking Your guidance and intervention. Strengthen my faith and fill me with joy and peace as I place my complete trust in You. In Jesus' name, amen.

Activate Today's Lesson:

1. Reflect on which of the three elements of breakthrough from Romans 12:12 you need to renew your commitment to today.

2. Identify and write down any lies from today's **"Lies to Reject"** that you've been struggling with. Cross them out symbolically to break their hold on your mind.

3. Write down below and begin to speak aloud a few of today's **"Daily Truths to Declare."** Believe that they are true and activated in your stand for restoration.

DAY 14
THE THREE ELEMENTS OF BREAKTHROUGH!

Today's Verse: Romans 12:12
Today's Reading: Pages 106 - 112

Your Marriage IS Getting Restored!

Today's Coloring Page:

"BE JOYFUL IN HOPE
PATIENT IN AFFLICTION
FAITHFUL IN PRAYER"
ROMANS 12:12

"From Coloring Your Stand" Coloring Book

Session 5 - Day 2

DAY 15 - THE PROCESS OF HOPE!

Romans 15:13 (NIV) "May the God of hope fill you with all joy and peace as you trust in him, so that you may overflow with hope by the power of the Holy Spirit."

Read pages 113 - 119: **DAY 15 - THE PROCESS OF HOPE!** from "40 Day Stand For Marriage Restoration."

Stand on this truth:

In Romans 15:13, we find a powerful promise: as we trust in God, He fills us with joy, peace, and overflowing hope through the Holy Spirit. **The God of Hope: Our God is the source of true hope.** Despite the challenges in our marriages, He offers us an abundance of hope, joy, and peace. **The Process of Trust: Trust is the conduit through which hope flows.** By placing our trust in God, we invite Him to fill us with supernatural joy and peace, leading to an overflow of hope. **Active Trust: Trusting God is an active, daily choice.** It involves surrendering our doubts and fears, aligning our actions with His promises, and inviting Him to work in and through us.

Prayer for Today:

"Heavenly Father, I come before You, the God of hope, seeking an outpouring of joy, peace, and hope in my stand for marriage restoration. Help me to trust You more deeply, surrendering my doubts and fears to Your care. Fill me with Your Holy Spirit, empowering me to walk in faith and hope, even in the midst of challenges. Renew my strength, guide my steps, and lead me toward reconciliation. In Jesus' name, amen.

Activate Today's Lesson:

1. Reflect on how well you trust God during this season of standing for marriage restoration. Are there any areas where God wants you to grow in trust?

2. Identify and write down any lies from today's **"Lies to Reject"** that you've been struggling with. Cross them out symbolically to break their hold on your mind.

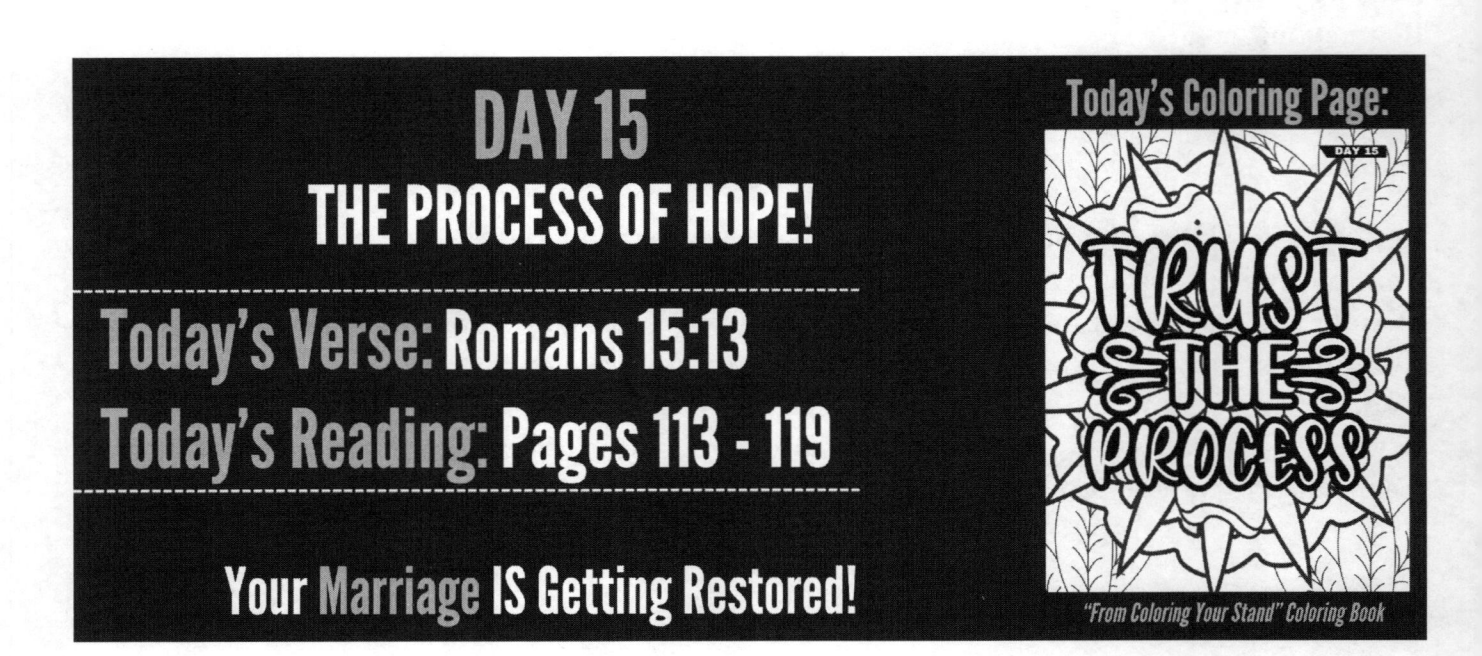

3. Write down below and begin to speak aloud a few of today's **"Daily Truths to Declare."** Believe that they are true and activated in your stand for restoration.

DAY 15
THE PROCESS OF HOPE!

Today's Verse: Romans 15:13
Today's Reading: Pages 113 - 119

Your Marriage IS Getting Restored!

Today's Coloring Page:

"From Coloring Your Stand" Coloring Book

Session 5 - Day 3

Day 16: The Price for Hope

Romans 8:24-25 (NIV) "For in this hope we were saved. But hope that is seen is no hope at all. Who hopes for what he already has? But if we hope for what we do not yet have, we wait for it patiently."

Read pages 120 – 126: **Day 16: The Price for Hope** from "40 Day Stand For Marriage Restoration."

Stand on this truth:

In Romans 8:24-25, we're reminded that genuine hope requires patience and trust in God's unseen work. As standers, we must be willing to pay the price of patiently waiting for the restoration of our marriages, even when we see no evidence of it.

Prayer for Today:

"Heavenly Father, I acknowledge the price of hope and the patience required as I wait for the restoration of my marriage. Help me to trust Your unseen work, knowing that Your timing is perfect. Strengthen my faith, Lord, and grant me the perseverance to endure this journey with hope and confidence in Your promises. May Your Spirit fill me with peace and assurance as I wait patiently for Your divine intervention. In Jesus' name, amen.

Activate Today's Lesson:

1. Reflect on your willingness to patiently wait for the restoration of your marriage. How could embracing the truth of the price for hope impact your stand?

2. Identify and write down any lies from today's **"Lies to Reject"** that you've been struggling with. Cross them out symbolically to break their hold on your mind.

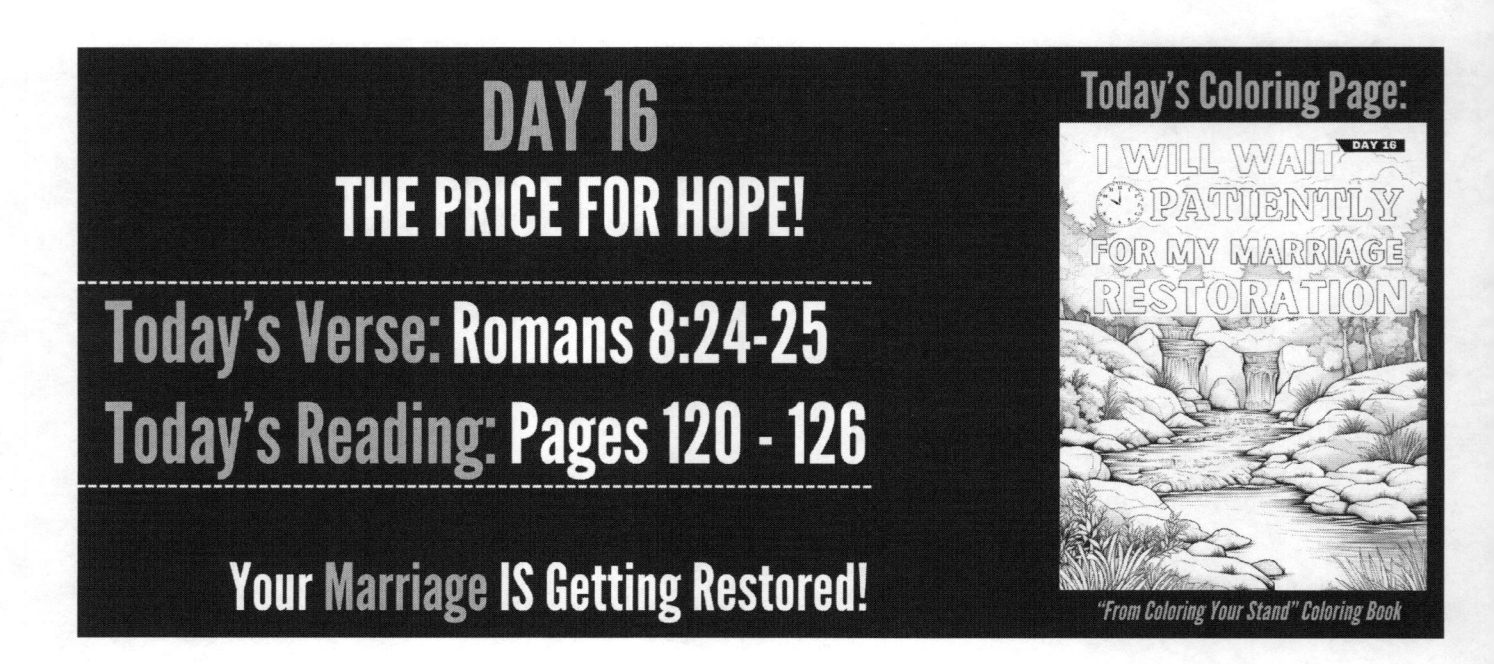

3. Write down below and begin to speak aloud a few of today's **"Daily Truths to Declare."** Believe that they are true and activated in your stand for restoration.

DAY 16
THE PRICE FOR HOPE!

Today's Verse: Romans 8:24-25
Today's Reading: Pages 120 - 126

Your Marriage IS Getting Restored!

Today's Coloring Page:
I WILL WAIT PATIENTLY FOR MY MARRIAGE RESTORATION

"From Coloring Your Stand" Coloring Book

Session 5 - Day 4

Day 19: Always Have Hope

Psalm 71:14 (NIV) "As for me, I will always have hope; I will praise you more and more."

Read pages 142 - 148: **Day 19: Always Have Hope** from "40 Day Stand For Marriage Restoration."

Stand on this truth:

It's easy to feel overwhelmed and hopeless. But as believers, we are called to cling to hope and trust in God's redemptive power, even when circumstances seem dire. Our hope is anchored not in what we see but in the unwavering faithfulness of our Heavenly Father. Do you find yourself grappling with feelings of helplessness and despair in your marriage? Despite the difficulties, Psalm 71:14 reminds us that we can always have hope in God and continually praise Him.

Prayer for Today:

"Heavenly Father, I come before You with a heart filled with hope and praise. Strengthen my faith and fill me with unwavering hope as I trust Your perfect plan for my marriage. Help me to fix my eyes on You and praise You even in the midst of difficulties. In Jesus' name, amen.

Activate Today's Lesson:

1. How can you cultivate a spirit of continuous praise, even in the midst of marital struggles?

2. Identify and write down any lies from today's **"Lies to Reject"** that you've been struggling with. Cross them out symbolically to break their hold on your mind.

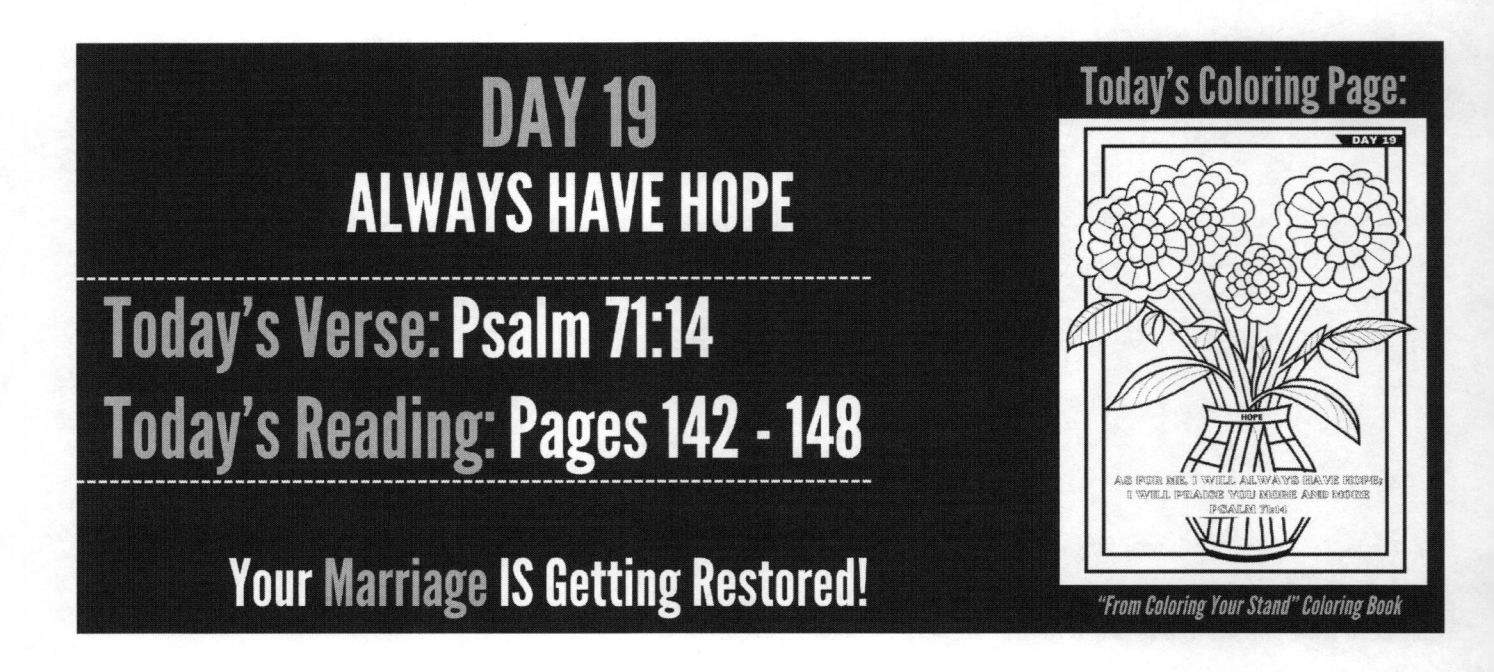

3. Write down below and begin to speak aloud a few of today's **"Daily Truths to Declare."** Believe that they are true and activated in your stand for restoration.

DAY 19
ALWAYS HAVE HOPE

Today's Verse: Psalm 71:14
Today's Reading: Pages 142 - 148

Your Marriage IS Getting Restored!

Today's Coloring Page:

"From Coloring Your Stand" Coloring Book

SESSION 5 - DAY 5

DAY 25: IT WILL BE GREATER THAN BEFORE

Haggai 2:9 (KJV) "The glory of this latter house shall be greater than of the former, saith the Lord of hosts: And in this place will I give peace, saith the Lord of hosts."

Read pages 186 - 192: **Day 25: IT WILL BE GREATER THAN BEFORE** from "40 Day Stand For Marriage Restoration."

Stand on this truth:

Haggai 2:9 reminds us that the glory of our latter days will surpass the former. This promise assures us that God is bringing greater restoration and renewal to our marriages. God's promise extends beyond physical structures to our spiritual, emotional, and relational lives, including our marriages. Just as He assured His people of a greater glory in the rebuilding of the temple, He promises greater restoration and renewal in our broken marriages.

Prayer for Today:

"Heavenly Father, I thank You for Your promise of restoration and renewal in my marriage. Help me keep my eyes fixed on Your promises rather than the scars of the past. Give me the faith to believe that You are making my marriage greater than ever. Fill me with Your peace and guide me in this journey of healing and transformation. Thank You for the goodness that is coming to my family. In Jesus' name, amen.

Activate Today's Lesson:

1. Consider how embracing the truth that "It Will Be Greater Than Before" could impact your stand for marriage restoration.

2. Identify and write down any lies from today's **"Lies to Reject"** that you've been struggling with. Cross them out symbolically to break their hold on your mind.

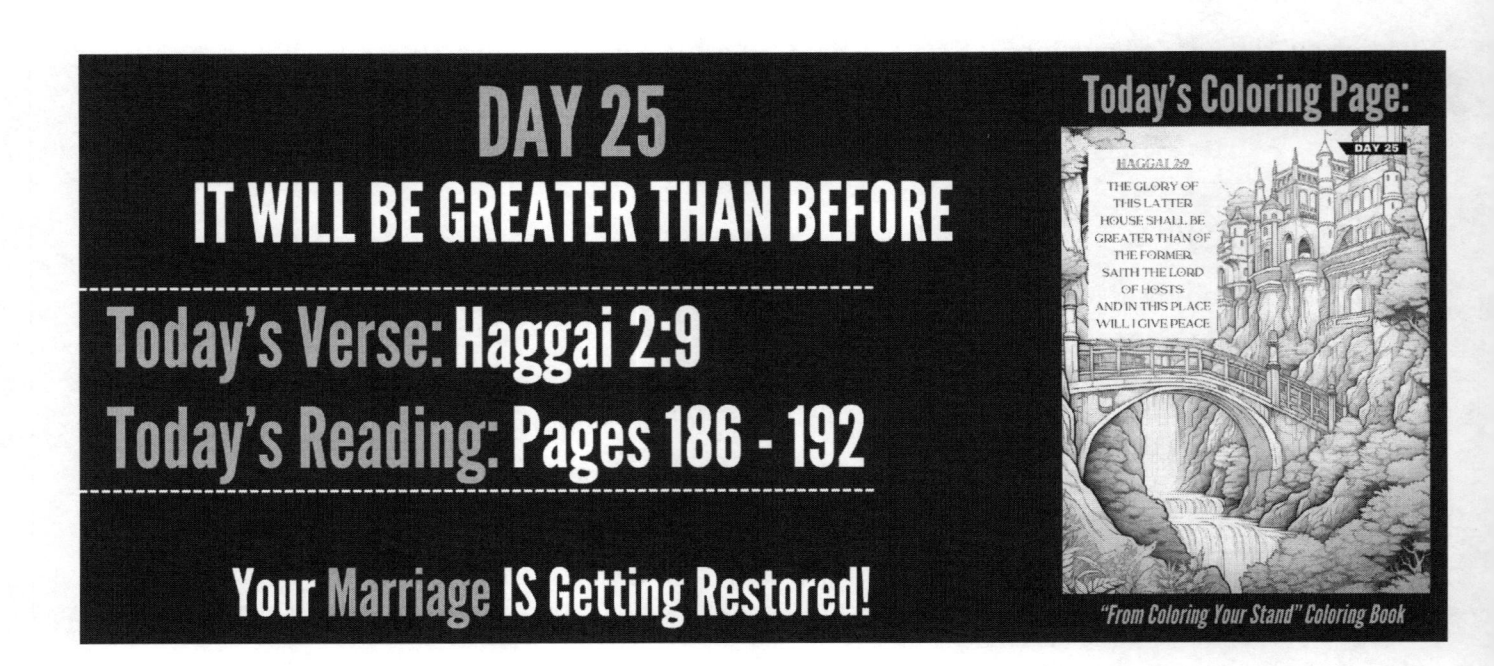

3. Write down below and begin to speak aloud a few of today's **"Daily Truths to Declare."** Believe that they are true and activated in your stand for restoration.

DAY 25

IT WILL BE GREATER THAN BEFORE

Today's Verse: **Haggai 2:9**

Today's Reading: **Pages 186 - 192**

Your Marriage IS Getting Restored!

Today's Coloring Page:

HAGGAI 2:9
THE GLORY OF THIS LATTER HOUSE SHALL BE GREATER THAN OF THE FORMER, SAITH THE LORD OF HOSTS, AND IN THIS PLACE WILL I GIVE PEACE

"From Coloring Your Stand" Coloring Book

SESSION 5 - DAY 6

REVIEWING THIS WEEK'S DAILY READINGS

Spend a few moments today reviewing last week's daily readings. You will have a chance to discuss these topics at the start of next week's group session. Writing these answers ahead of time will best prepare you for next week's opening group time discussion.

What encouraging takeaways did you have from this day's reading? What specific thoughts, verses, lies, declarations, or testimonies are specifically impactful for your stand?

Day 1 – "Day 14: The Three Elements of Breakthrough" insights:

Day 2 – "Day 15: The Process of Hope!" insights:

Day 3 – "Day 16: The Price for Hope!" **insights:**

Day 4 – "Day 19: Always Have Hope" insights:

Day 5 – "Day 25: It Will Be Greater Than Before" insights:

Write this week's Memory Verse below:

Additional Notes:

Session 6 - Standing Aware of the Enemy's Plans

In session 6, "Standing Aware of the Enemy's Plans," Pastor Jason Carver exposes the predictable tactics the enemy uses to discourage and derail believers standing for marriage restoration. You will learn how to recognize and resist the lies of the enemy, including fear, doubt, and discouragement. Pastor Jason highlights the importance of relying on spiritual weapons, not worldly strategies, to overcome the attacks against your marriage. Using biblical examples, he encourages you to stay focused on God's work and refuse to be distracted or drawn down by the enemy's schemes.

"We cannot wage war according to the flesh. Our weapons are not of human effort but come from God's supernatural spiritual armory. Speculations and 'what if' scenarios are the number one way the enemy attacks you. These are negative, demonically inspired thoughts that lead to fear and doubt. We must take every thought captive to the obedience of Christ and not let these speculations undermine our faith and hope." – Jason Carver

Discussion and review from last week's daily readings of "40 Day Stand For Marriage Restoration."

Before you begin this week's teaching video, go around the group and discuss your insights and takeaways from each of the daily readings from last week. Revisit last week's Day 6 Workbook page for an overview of your reading takeaways.

Write any insights from other group members below:

Any specific day from last week's reading that you need to go back and read again?

Before you begin this week's Video Teaching, pray for the Holy Spirit to come and bring revelation to your stand for restoration as you watch this week's teaching.

Follow along with this week's teaching video and fill in the blanks below as the answers appear on the screen.

Session 6 — VIDEO GUIDE
STANDING FOR MARRIAGE RESTORATION

1) We must become _____ of the devil's schemes to undermine our stand for restoration.

2) Our weapons are not of _____ effort but come from God's supernatural spiritual armory.

3) God has given _____ divine power to break down the _____ standing against your marriage.

4) Don't let the enemy lure you into fighting with _____ tactics. Remember, your battle is spiritual, and your weapons must be _____ too!

5) The enemy uses _____ to attack us by planting '_____ ____' scenarios – negative, demonically inspired thoughts that lead to fear and doubt.

6) _____ _____ are those things we perceive as _____ than God's power to solve, designed to make us doubt God's ability or desire to heal.

7) If you go down to the Valley of Ono, you will quickly find yourself saying _____ _____!

8) When tempted to go down, remind yourself: 'I am doing a _____ _____ for my family, and I cannot afford to stop now!'

9) When standing against the attacks of the enemy, you often don't need '_____' actions, but '_____' actions.

10) Never forget, that you can know the enemy's _____ coming against your restoration, and you possess divine power to _____ them!

Discussion Questions from This Week's Teaching Video

Question #1: Why is it crucial to recognize that our weapons are not of human effort but come from God's supernatural spiritual armory? How can relying on spiritual weapons change the way we approach challenges in our marriage restoration?

Question #2: Jason shared a list of Examples of Waging War "in the flesh" for Your Marriage. How easy is it to be tempted to wage war in the flesh during this difficult time of standing for your marriage? Have you been encouraged by anyone to use any of these "worldly tactics?"

Question #3: How do speculations and 'what if' scenarios create fear and doubt in our minds? How can you identify and take captive these thoughts to prevent them from undermining your faith and hope?

Question #4: What are some examples of "lofty things" that try to appear greater than God's power to heal? How can recognizing these thoughts as attacks help you to trust more fully in God's ability and desire to heal?

Question #5: During your stand for marriage restoration, you'll encounter opportunities to descend into a valley of negativity, retaliation, and despair. The Valley of Ono represents the temptation to respond to your spouse in ways that don't align with God's character. How often are you tempted to be drawn into negativity, retaliation, and destructive behavior?

Question #6: Why might it be more effective to focus on renewing your current actions rather than seeking new ones when standing against the attacks of the enemy? How can consistency in your responses help you in your journey of restoration?

Question #7: Jason listed, "Ten thoughts we should immediately take captive." Go around the group and declare: *"I take captive the thought that..."*

1. "I take captive the thought that our problems are too big for God to fix."

2. "I take captive the thought that I'm just fooling myself about restoration."

3. "I take captive the thought that my situation is unique and beyond help."

4. "I take captive the thought that I must have done something unforgivable."

5. "I take captive the thought that the future is uncertain; I can't trust God to handle it."

6. "I take captive the thought that everyone will judge me if I continue standing for my marriage."

7. "I take captive the thought that it's better to protect myself and not risk getting hurt again."

8. "I take captive the thought that maybe this is a sign that I'm meant to be with someone else."

9. "I take captive the thought that I'm just wasting my time; this will never work out."

10. "I take captive the thought that the more I try, the worse it gets; maybe it's a sign to give up."

This Week's Memory Verse

- 2 Corinthians 10:4 (NASB) *"for the weapons of our warfare are not of the flesh....., but divinely powerful for the destruction of fortresses."*

- (Bonus memory verses) – 2 Corinthians 10:5 (NASB) *"We are destroying speculations and every lofty thing raised up against the knowledge of God, and we are taking every thought captive to the obedience of Christ,"*

This Week's Daily Readings from "40 Day Stand for Marriage Restoration"

- *Day 1:* **"DAY 21 – NOT WON IN THE FLESH"** *(Pages 156 – 162)*
- *Day 2:* **"DAY 22 – DESTROYING SPECULATIONS"** *(Pages 163 – 169)*
- *Day 3:* **"DAY 23 – DESTROYING LOFTY THINGS"** *(Pages 170 – 177)*
- *Day 4:* **"DAY 34 – VISITING THE VALLEY OF ONO"** *(Pages 254 – 261)*
- *Day 5:* **"DAY 36 – NOT BY MIGHT, BUT BY MY SPIRIT!"** *(Pages 270 – 277)*

Scriptures From This Week's Video Teaching

2 Corinthians 2:11 (NLT) "so that Satan will not outsmart us. For we are familiar with his evil schemes."

2 Corinthians 2:11 (MSG) "After all, we don't want to unwittingly give Satan an opening for yet more mischief—we're not oblivious to his sly ways!"

Galatians 6:9 (NIV) "Let us not become weary in doing good, for at the proper time we will reap a harvest if we do not give up."

2 Corinthians 10:4 (NASB) "for the weapons of our warfare are not of the flesh....., but divinely powerful for the destruction of fortresses."

2 Corinthians 10:5 (NASB) "We are destroying speculations and every lofty thing raised up against the knowledge of God, and we are taking every thought captive to the obedience of Christ,"

Nehemiah 6:1–2 (NKJV) "[1]Now it happened when Sanballat, Tobiah, Geshem the Arab, and the rest of our enemies heard that I had rebuilt the wall, and that there were no breaks left in it (though at that time I had not hung the doors in the gates), [2]that Sanballat and Geshem sent to me, saying, "Come, let us meet together among the villages in the plain of Ono." But they thought to do me harm."

Nehemiah 6:3 (NKJV) "So I sent messengers to them, saying, "I am doing a great work, so that I cannot come down. Why should the work cease while I leave it and go down to you?""

Nehemiah 6:4 (NKJV) "But they sent me this message four times, and I answered them in the same manner."

Session 6 - Day 1

Day 21: Not Won in the Flesh

2 Corinthians 10:3-4 (ESV) "For though we walk in the flesh, we are not waging war according to the flesh. For the weapons of our warfare are not of the flesh but have divine power to destroy strongholds."

Read pages 156 - 162: **Day 21: NOT WON IN THE FLESH** from "40 Day Stand For Marriage Restoration."

Stand on this truth:

In our pursuit to see our marriages restored, it's common to resort to worldly methods and strategies. However, **2 Corinthians 10:3-4** reminds us that our battle is not fought in the flesh but with divine power that can demolish spiritual strongholds. Have you found yourself attempting to win back your spouse using worldly tactics? Despite our efforts, these methods often fall short. It's time to recognize that our fight for marriage restoration is spiritual, requiring divine power and heavenly weapons.

Prayer for Today:

"Heavenly Father, I acknowledge that my battle for marriage restoration is not fought in the flesh but with divine power. Help me let go of my dependence on worldly strategies and embrace the weapons of the Spirit. Fill me with Your wisdom, discernment, and faith as I pray, worship, and study Your Word. I trust You to bring forth supernatural restoration and transformation. In Jesus' name, amen."

Activate Today's Lesson:

1. How can you cultivate a spirit of continuous reliance on divine power, even in the midst of marital struggles?

2. Identify and write down any lies from today's **"Lies to Reject"** that you've been struggling with. Cross them out symbolically to break their hold on your mind.

3. Write down below and begin to speak aloud a few of today's **"Daily Truths to Declare."** Believe that they are true and activated in your stand for restoration.

DAY 21
NOT WON IN THE FLESH

Today's Verse: 2 Corinthians 10:3-4
Today's Reading: Pages 156 - 162

Your Marriage IS Getting Restored!

Today's Coloring Page:

"From Coloring Your Stand" Coloring Book

Session 6 - Day 2

Day 22: Destroying Speculations

2 Corinthians 10:4-5 (NASB) "For the weapons of our warfare are not of the flesh, but divinely powerful for the destruction of fortresses. We are destroying speculations and every lofty thing raised up against the knowledge of God, and we are taking every thought captive to the obedience of Christ."

Read pages 163 - 169: **Day 22: Destroying Speculations** from "40 Day Stand For Marriage Restoration."

Stand on this truth:

In our ongoing battle for the restoration of our marriages, it's essential to understand the stronghold of negative speculations and how they can hinder our faith and hope. Do you find yourself grappling with negative "what if" scenarios and speculations about your marriage? Today's passage reminds us of the importance of demolishing these strongholds and taking every thought captive to Christ.

Prayer for Today:

"Heavenly Father, I come before You burdened by negative speculations and strongholds in my mind regarding the restoration of my marriage. Help me take every thought captive and align them with Your truth. Grant me the strength to resist doubt and renew my faith in Your power to work miracles. In Jesus' name, amen."

Activate Today's Lesson:

1. How often have negative speculations invaded your mind regarding your marriage? How could demolishing these speculations impact your stand for restoration?

2. Identify and write down any lies from today's **"Lies to Reject"** that you've been struggling with. Cross them out symbolically to break their hold on your mind.

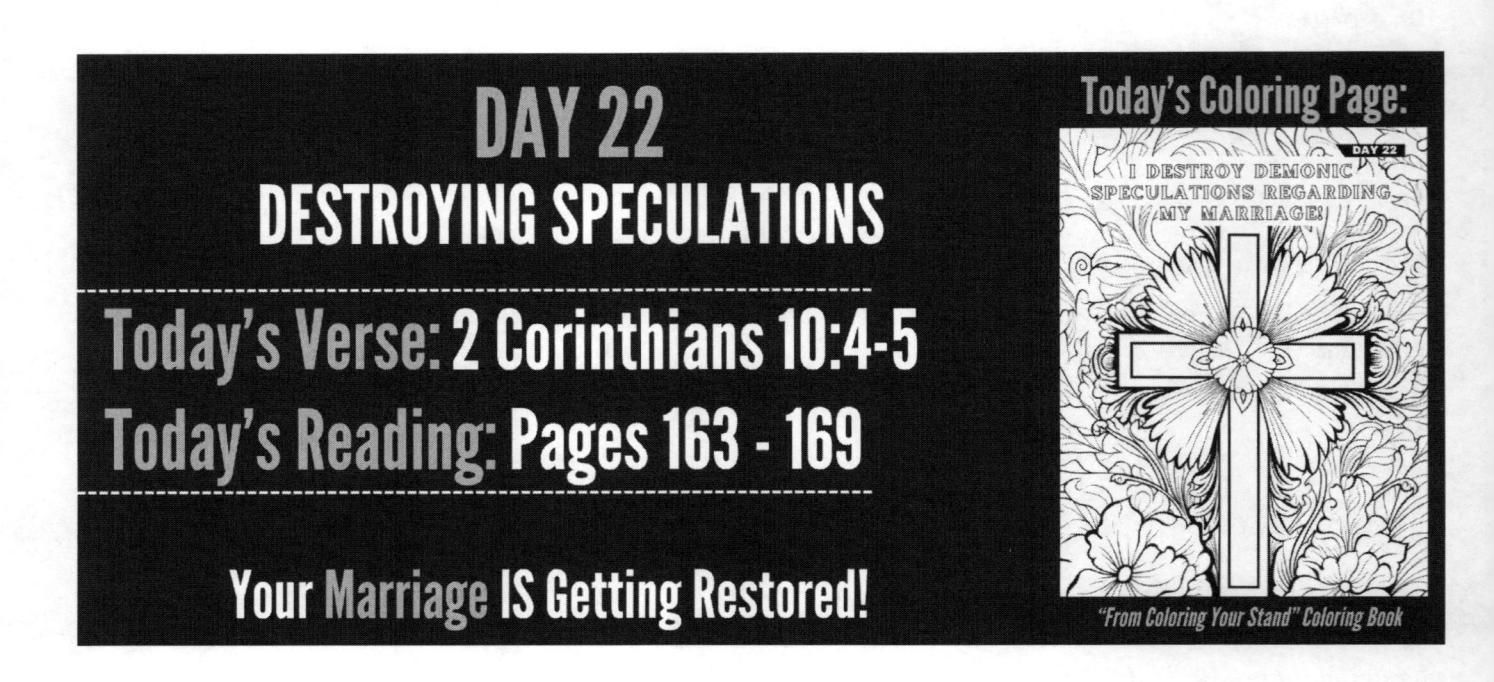

3. Write down below and begin to speak aloud a few of today's **"Daily Truths to Declare."** Believe that they are true and activated in your stand for restoration.

DAY 22
DESTROYING SPECULATIONS

Today's Verse: 2 Corinthians 10:4-5
Today's Reading: Pages 163 - 169

Your Marriage IS Getting Restored!

Today's Coloring Page:
I DESTROY DEMONIC SPECULATIONS REGARDING MY MARRIAGE!

"From Coloring Your Stand" Coloring Book

Session 6 - Day 3

Day 23: Destroying Lofty Things

2 Corinthians 10:5 (NASB) "We are destroying speculations and every lofty thing raised up against the knowledge of God, and we are taking every thought captive to the obedience of Christ."

Read pages 170 - 177: **Day 23: Destroying Lofty Things** from "40 Day Stand For Marriage Restoration."

Stand on this truth:

In our pursuit of marital restoration, it's essential to recognize and demolish every thought and belief that suggests our problems are too big for God to handle. Do you ever find yourself doubting God's ability to heal your marriage? Today's passage reminds us to confront and dismantle every thought that exalts itself above the power and wisdom of God.

Prayer for Today:

"Heavenly Father, I come before You, acknowledging any presence of lofty thoughts and strongholds in my mind regarding the restoration of my marriage. Help me surrender these doubts and fears to You, trusting in Your infinite wisdom and power. Renew my faith and strengthen me to resist any notion that diminishes Your greatness. In Jesus' name, amen."

Activate Today's Lesson:

1. How often are you tempted to believe that your marriage problems are too big for God to handle? How could embracing the truth of destroying lofty things impact your stand for restoration?

2. Identify and write down any lies from today's **"Lies to Reject"** that you've been struggling with. Cross them out symbolically to break their hold on your mind.

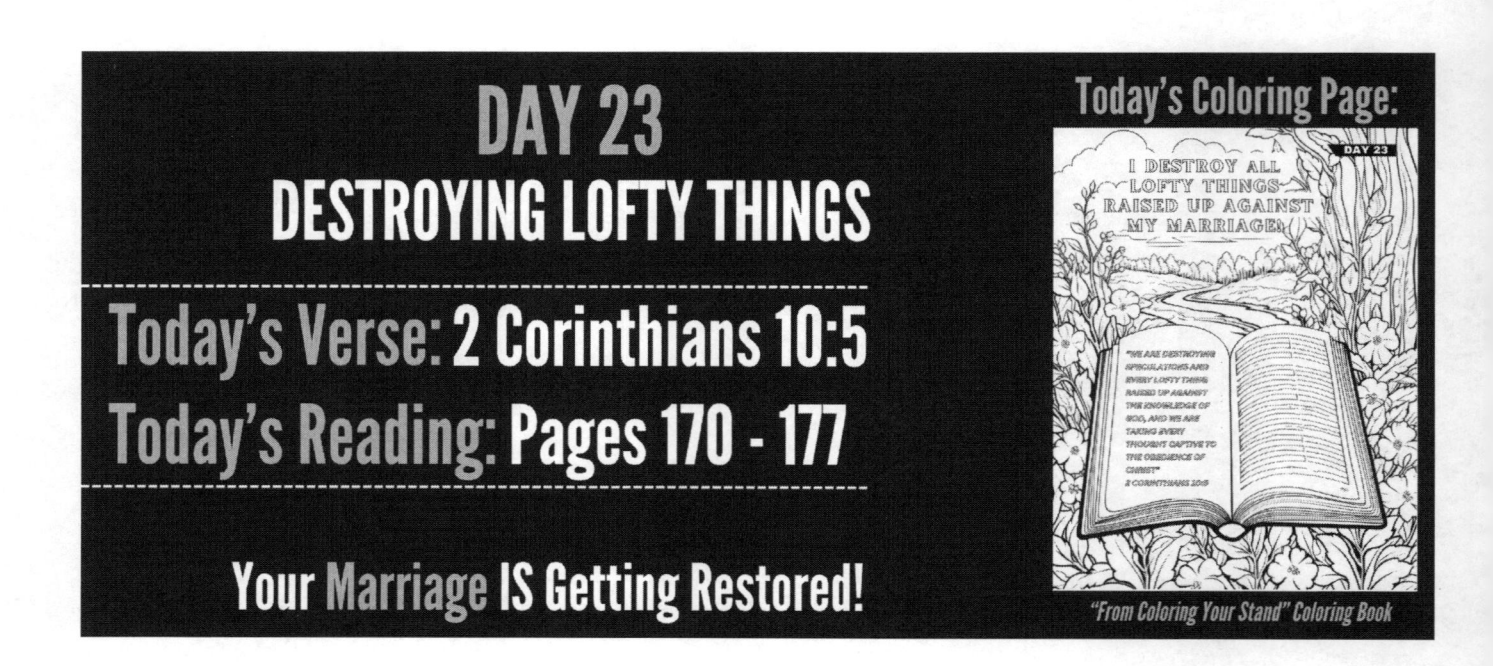

3. Write down below and begin to speak aloud a few of today's **"Daily Truths to Declare."** Believe that they are true and activated in your stand for restoration.

DAY 23
DESTROYING LOFTY THINGS

Today's Verse: 2 Corinthians 10:5
Today's Reading: Pages 170 - 177

Your Marriage IS Getting Restored!

Today's Coloring Page:

"From Coloring Your Stand" Coloring Book

SESSION 6 - DAY 4

DAY 34: THE VALLEY OF ONO

Nehemiah 6:2 (ESV) "Sanballat and Geshem sent to me, saying, 'Come and let us meet together at Hakkephirim in the plain of Ono.' But they intended to do me harm."

Read pages 254 - 261: **Day 34: The Valley of Ono** from "40 Day Stand For Marriage Restoration."

Stand on this truth:

In Nehemiah 6:2, we see how Nehemiah's enemies tried to lure him down to the Valley of Ono, a place of harm and destruction. Similarly, during our stand for marriage restoration, we'll encounter opportunities to descend into a valley of negativity, retaliation, and despair. The Valley of Ono represents a temptation to respond to our spouse in ways that don't align with God's character. It's a place where we're drawn into negativity, retaliation, and destructive behavior.

Prayer for Today:

"Heavenly Father, thank you for reminding me that I don't have to descend into the valley of negativity and retaliation. Help me to stay strong in my faith, recognizing the enemy's tactics and resisting them with courage. Forgive me for any past moments of weakness, and guide me back to the path of restoration. May your victory be evident in my marriage. In Jesus' name, I pray. Amen."

Activate Today's Lesson:

1. How does embracing the truth about visiting the Valley of Ono impact your stand for marriage restoration?

2. Identify and write down any lies from today's **"Lies to Reject"** that you've been struggling with. Cross them out symbolically to break their hold on your mind.

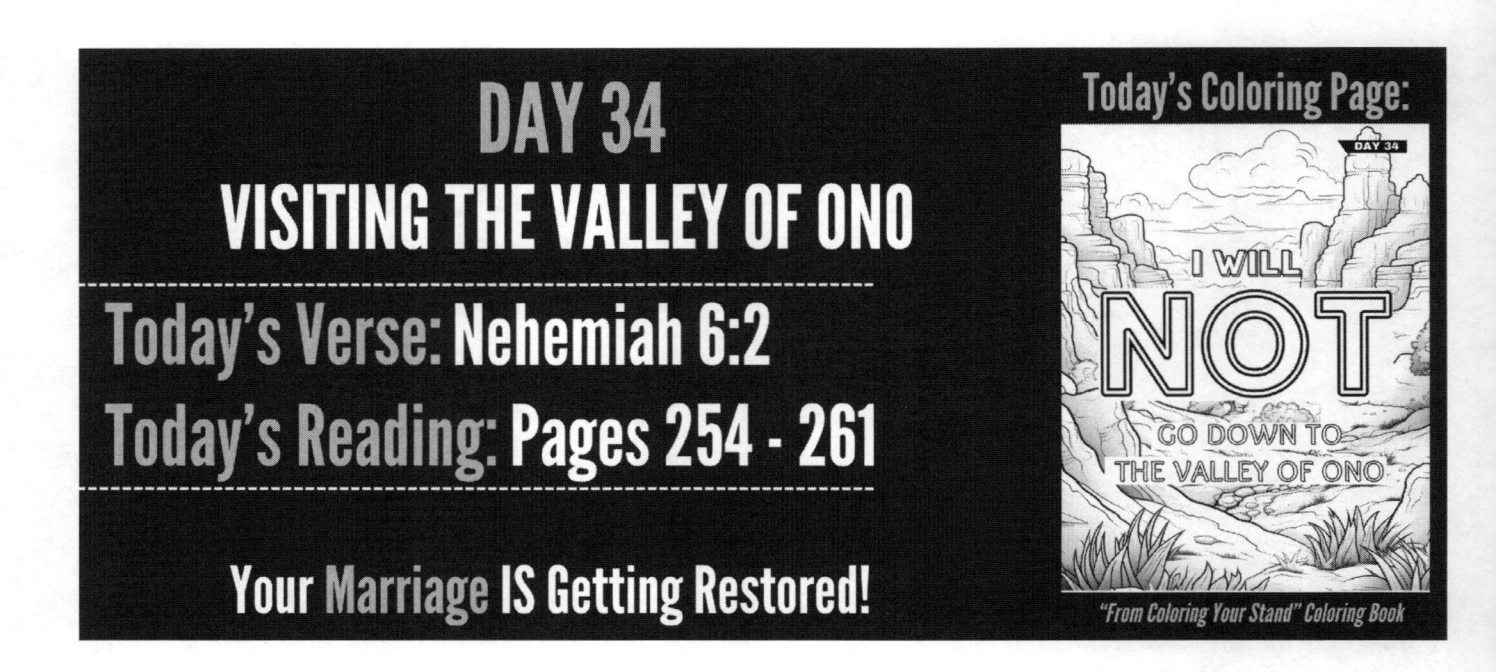

3. Write down below and begin to speak aloud a few of today's **"Daily Truths to Declare."** Believe that they are true and activated in your stand for restoration.

DAY 34
VISITING THE VALLEY OF ONO

Today's Verse: Nehemiah 6:2
Today's Reading: Pages 254 - 261

Your Marriage IS Getting Restored!

Today's Coloring Page:

I WILL NOT GO DOWN TO THE VALLEY OF ONO

"From Coloring Your Stand" Coloring Book

SESSION 6 - DAY 5

DAY 36: NOT BY MIGHT, BUT BY HIS SPIRIT!

Zechariah 4:6 (ESV) "Then he said to me, 'This is the word of the Lord to Zerubbabel: Not by might, nor by power, but by my Spirit, says the Lord of hosts.'"

Read pages 270 - 277: **Day 36: Not by might, but by His Spirit!** from "40 Day Stand For Marriage Restoration."

Stand on this truth:

Zerubbabel, a key figure in God's restoration plan for Israel, teaches us an important lesson about reliance on God's Spirit. Just as Zerubbabel depended on divine intervention to rebuild Jerusalem, we, too, must trust in the power of God's Spirit to restore our marriages. This profound message reminds us that true transformation and restoration in our marriages come not from our own strength or efforts but from the power of God's Spirit.

Prayer for Today:

"Heavenly Father, I acknowledge that true restoration in my marriage comes not from my own might or strength but from Your Spirit. Help me to surrender my efforts and trust in Your supernatural power to work in my life and relationship. May Your Spirit lead, guide, and empower us as we seek restoration. In Jesus' name, amen."

Activate Today's Lesson:

1. How has relying on your own strength impacted your stand for marriage restoration?

2. Identify and write down any lies from today's **"Lies to Reject"** that you've been struggling with. Cross them out symbolically to break their hold on your mind.

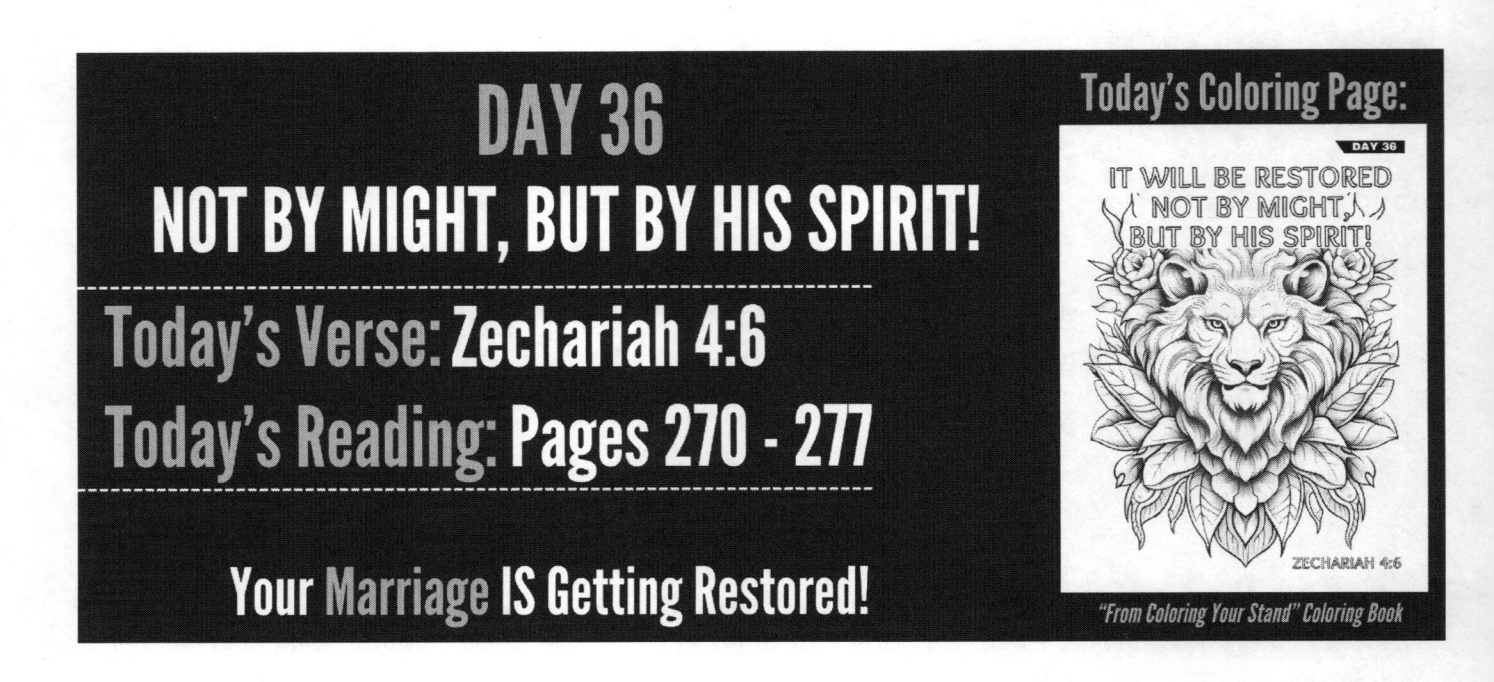

3. Write down below and begin to speak aloud a few of today's **"Daily Truths to Declare."** Believe that they are true and activated in your stand for restoration.

DAY 36

NOT BY MIGHT, BUT BY HIS SPIRIT!

Today's Verse: **Zechariah 4:6**

Today's Reading: **Pages 270 - 277**

Your Marriage IS Getting Restored!

Today's Coloring Page:

"From Coloring Your Stand" Coloring Book

SESSION 6 - DAY 6

REVIEWING THIS WEEK'S DAILY READINGS

Spend a few moments today reviewing last week's daily readings. You will have a chance to discuss these topics at the start of next week's group session. Writing these answers ahead of time will best prepare you for next week's opening group time discussion.

What encouraging takeaways did you have from this day's reading? What specific thoughts, verses, lies, declarations, or testimonies are specifically impactful for your stand?

Day 1 – "Day 21: Not won in the flesh" insights:

Day 2 – "Day 22: Destroying speculations" insights:

Day 3 – "Day 23: Destroying lofty things" insights:

Day 4 – "Day 34: The Valley of Ono" insights

Day 5 – "Day 36: Not by might, but by His Spirit!" insights:

Write this week's Memory Verse below:

Additional Notes:

Session 7 - Standing With The Divine Perspective

In session 7, "Standing With the Divine Perspective," Pastor Jason Carver challenges you to shift your focus from earthly circumstances to God's heavenly perspective. He explains the importance of renewing your mind through scripture and intentionally choosing to see your marriage through God's eyes. By focusing on His promises rather than the problems, you will find clarity, hope, and strength for the journey. Pastor Jason encourages you to trust in God's sovereignty, reminding you that nothing is impossible for Him and that He is working, even when you cannot see it.

"The most important aspect of standing for marriage restoration is to stand with a divine perspective. The divine perspective sets its mind on God's ability to pursue and touch our spouses. When we have the perspective of heaven, we have a greater confidence, a greater reality that God is actually moving right now." – Jason Carver

<u>Discussion and review from last week's daily readings of "40 Day Stand For Marriage Restoration."</u>

Before you begin this week's teaching video, go around the group and discuss your insights and takeaways from each of the daily readings from last week. Revisit last week's Day 6 Workbook page for an overview of your reading takeaways.

Write any insights from other group members below:

Any specific day from last week's reading that you need to go back and read again?

Before you begin this week's Video Teaching, pray for the Holy Spirit to come and bring revelation to your stand for restoration as you watch this week's teaching.

Follow along with this week's teaching video and fill in the blanks below as the answers appear on the screen.

Session 7 — **VIDEO GUIDE** — **STANDING FOR MARRIAGE RESTORATION**

1) Way too many standers are _____ led and not _____ led.

2) The most important aspect of standing for your marriage restoration is to stand with a _____ _____.

3) A major element of standing with a Divine Perspective is _____ what you _____ on.

4) The Divine Perspective focuses on _____ faithfulness, not your _____ attitude or actions.

5) The Divine Perspective knows the power of being _____ while standing _____.

6) The sitting season is an invitation to surrender _____ and allow God to reveal His power and glory.

7) Be Supernaturally _____ regarding the promises of God.

8) The Divine Perspective sets its mind to God's _____ to _____ and _____ our spouse!

9) Know that God is _____ your spouse even if they are not pursuing Him.

10) God's holy _____ is actively at work in your spouse's life, purifying them from their sins, doubts, and struggles they are facing.

11) The Divine Perspective sets its mind to the truth that God is releasing the _____ to fight for your marriage!

12) Pray that the _____-_____ angel will deliver that same message to your spouse, reassuring them that they need not fear returning to the marriage.

Discussion Questions from This Week's Teaching Video

Question #1: Jason mentioned that way too many standers are spouse-led and not Spirit-led; how much can you relate to this? How can focusing on God's faithfulness rather than your spouse's attitude or actions help you maintain a positive and hopeful outlook? How can this perspective help you move forward in your stand?

Question #2: How have your thoughts affected your emotions and feelings while standing, and can you see how those feelings drove your actions, or lack thereof?

Question #3: What does it mean to you to be still while standing firm for marriage restoration? How might you practice stillness and firmness in your current situation? What would that look like to you?

Question #4: What do you think God was saying to Jason when he said to be supernaturally stubborn regarding the promises of God? How can you cultivate this kind of "stubbornness" in your own stand for marriage restoration?

Question #5: Read Isaiah 65:1-2. How does knowing that God is pursuing your spouse, even if they are not pursuing Him, influence your hope and prayers? Can you think of examples in your own life where this truth has been evident?

Question #6: How does believing that God's holy fire is actively at work in your spouse's life, purifying them from their sins and struggles while also protecting them, affect your prayers and faith? Have you seen any signs of this purification and protection process in either their or your own life?

Question #7: How comfortable are you in believing that God is releasing the supernatural to fight for your marriage? Can you share any instances where you have witnessed God's supernatural intervention in your life?

Question #8: What do you think about praying for the divorce-busting angel to deliver a message to your spouse? If comfortable, go around in your group and ask God to send this angel to each of your spouses right now!

This Week's Memory Verse

- *Colossians 3:2 (NIV)* – "*Set your minds on things above, not on earthly things.*"

- **(Bonus memory verses)** - *Isaiah 65:1–2 (NIV)* "*I revealed myself to those who did not ask for me; I was found by those who did not seek me. To a nation that did not call on my name, I said, 'Here am I, here am I.'* "

This Week's Daily Readings from "40 Day Stand for Marriage Restoration"

- *Day 1:* "**DAY 29 - STAND WITH A DIVINE PERSPECTIVE**" (Pages 215 - 222)

- *Day 2:* "**DAY 31 - THE SITTING SEASON**" (Pages 230 - 237)

- *Day 3:* "**DAY 32 - JUST STAND FIRM AND DON'T GIVE UP!**" (Pages 238 - 245)

- *Day 4:* "**DAY 26 - A WALL OF FIRE IS SURROUNDING YOUR SPOUSE**" (Pages 193 - 199)

- *Day 5:* "**DAY 11 - INVITE THE DIVORCE-BUSTING ANGEL TO YOUR MARRIAGE**" (Pages 82 - 89)

Scriptures From This Week's Video Teaching

Colossians 3:2 (NIV) "*Set your minds on things above, not on earthly things.*"

Romans 12:2 (NIV) "*Do not conform any longer to the pattern of this world, but be transformed by the renewing of your mind. Then you will be able to test and approve what God's will is--his good, pleasing and perfect will.*"

Psalm 2:4 (ESV) "*He who sits in the heavens laughs; the Lord holds them in derision.*"

Luke 1:37 (ESV) "*For nothing will be impossible with God.*"

Job 9:10 (NIV) "*He performs wonders that cannot be fathomed, miracles that cannot be counted.*"

Jeremiah 32:27 (NIV) "*I am the LORD, the God of all mankind. Is anything too hard for me?*"

Isaiah 43:19 (NLT) "*For I am about to do something new. See, I have already begun! Do you not see it? I will make a pathway through the wilderness. I will create rivers in the dry wasteland.*"

Zechariah 4:6 (ESV) "*Then he said to me, "This is the word of the Lord to Zerubbabel: Not by might, nor by power, but by my Spirit, says the Lord of hosts.*"

John 11:40 (NKJV) "*Did I not say to you that if you would believe you would see the glory of God?*"

Exodus 14:13–14 (NIV) "Moses answered the people, "Do not be afraid. Stand firm and you will see the deliverance the Lord will bring you today. The Egyptians you see today you will never see again. ¹⁴The Lord will fight for you; you need only to be still."

Psalm 46:10 (NIV) "Be still, and know that I am God; I will be exalted among the nations, I will be exalted in the earth."

Isaiah 30:15 (NIV) "This is what the Sovereign Lord, the Holy One of Israel, says: "In repentance and <u>rest</u> is your salvation, in <u>quietness</u> and trust is your strength, but you would have none of it."

2 Chronicles 20:17 (NIV) "You will not have to fight this battle. Take up your positions; stand firm and see the deliverance the Lord will give you, O Judah and Jerusalem. Do not be afraid; do not be discouraged. Go out to face them tomorrow, and the Lord will be with you.'

Ephesians 6:13 (AMP) "Therefore put on God's complete armor, that you may be able to resist and stand your ground on the evil day [of danger], and, having done all [the crisis demands], to stand [firmly in your place]."

Galatians 6:9 (NIV) "Let us not become weary in doing good, for at the proper time we will reap a harvest if we do not give up."

Isaiah 65:1–2 (NIV) "I revealed myself to those who did not ask for me; I was found by those who did not seek me. To a nation that did not call on my name, I said, 'Here am I, here am I.' ²All day long I have held out my hands to an obstinate people, who walk in ways not good, pursuing their own imaginations—

Romans 10:20–21 (NIV) "And Isaiah boldly says, "I was found by those who did not seek me; I revealed myself to those who did not ask for me.²¹But concerning Israel he says, "All day long I have held out my hands to a disobedient and obstinate people."

Zechariah 2:5 (NASB) "'For I,' declares the Lord, 'will be a wall of fire around her, and I will be the glory in her midst.'"

Malachi 3:3 (NIV) "He will sit as a refiner and purifier of silver; he will purify the Levites and refine them like gold and silver. Then the Lord will have men who will bring offerings in righteousness,"

1 Peter 2:9 (NIV) "But you are a chosen people, a royal priesthood, a holy nation, a people belonging to God, that you may declare the praises of him who called you out of darkness into his wonderful light."

Matthew 1:19–20 (ESV) "And her husband Joseph, being a just man and unwilling to put her to shame, resolved to divorce her quietly. ²⁰But as he considered these things, behold, an angel of the Lord appeared to him in a dream, saying, "Joseph, son of David, do not fear to take Mary as your wife, for that which is conceived in her is from the Holy Spirit."

Matthew 1:24 (ESV) "When Joseph woke from sleep, he did as the angel of the Lord commanded him: he took his wife,"

Hebrews 1:14 (NIV) "Are not all angels ministering spirits sent to serve those who will inherit salvation?"

Session 7 - Day 1

DAY 29 - STAND WITH A DIVINE PERSPECTIVE

Colossians 3:2 (ESV) "Set your minds on things that are above, not on things that are on earth."

Read pages 215 - 222: **DAY 29 - STAND WITH A DIVINE PERSPECTIVE** from "40 Day Stand For Marriage Restoration."

Stand on this truth:

It's easy to become consumed by the visible struggles and obstacles that surround us. However, as standers, we are called to rise above the natural and adopt a divine perspective, one that aligns with Heaven's view of our situations. God calls us to set our minds on heavenly things rather than earthly concerns. This shift in perspective enables us to see beyond the limitations of our circumstances and anchor our hope in His unfailing love and power.

Prayer for Today:

"Heavenly Father, help me to adopt a divine perspective and set my mind on things above. Grant me the strength to view my spouse and my marriage through Your eyes with love, grace, and compassion. Fill me with unwavering hope and faith, knowing that Your plan for my marriage far exceeds what I can perceive. Guide me in walking by faith and not by sight, trusting in Your divine view for restoration. In Jesus' name, I pray. Amen."

Activate Today's Lesson:

1. How does adopting a divine perspective impact your stand for marriage restoration?

2. Identify and write down any lies from today's **"Lies to Reject"** that you've been struggling with. Cross them out symbolically to break their hold on your mind.

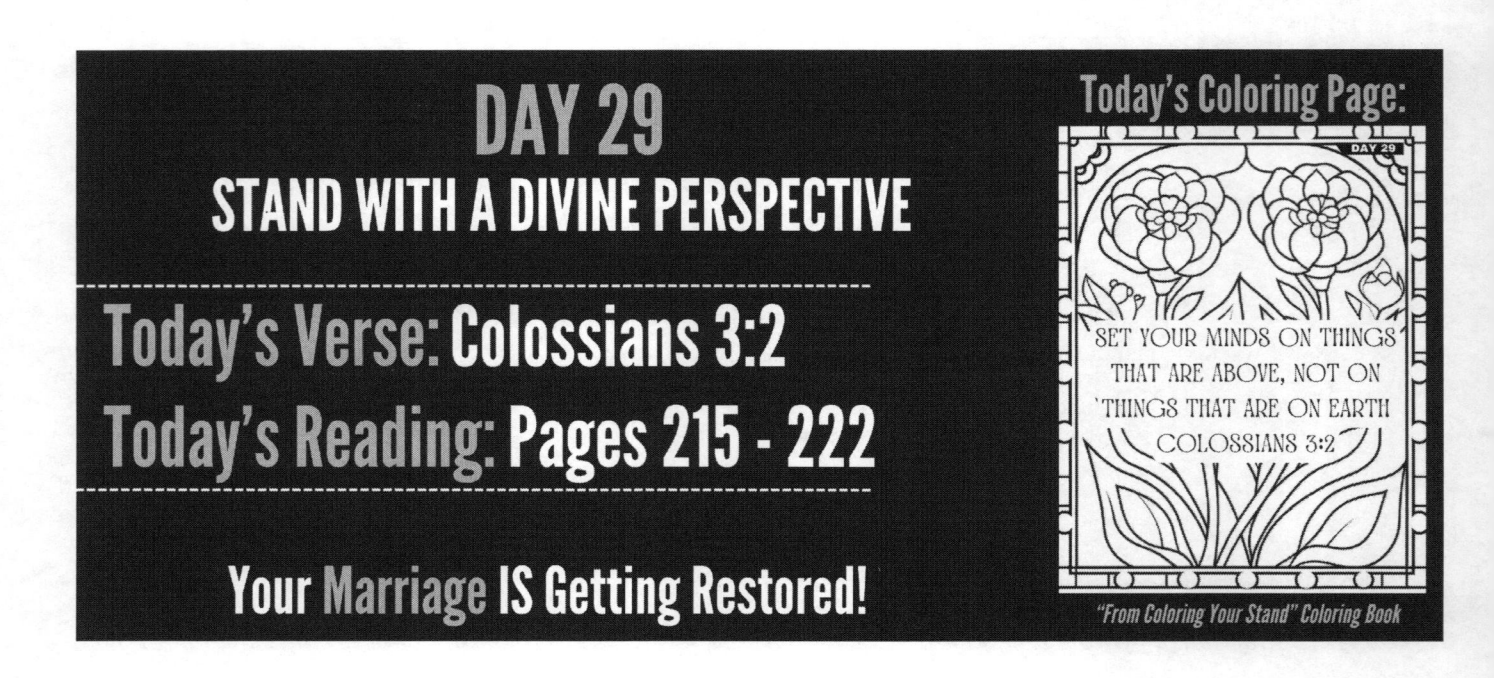

3. Write down below and begin to speak aloud a few of today's **"Daily Truths to Declare."** Believe that they are true and activated in your stand for restoration.

DAY 29
STAND WITH A DIVINE PERSPECTIVE

Today's Verse: Colossians 3:2
Today's Reading: Pages 215 - 222

Your Marriage IS Getting Restored!

Today's Coloring Page:

SET YOUR MINDS ON THINGS THAT ARE ABOVE, NOT ON THINGS THAT ARE ON EARTH
COLOSSIANS 3:2

"From Coloring Your Stand" Coloring Book

Session 7 - Day 2

DAY 31 - THE SITTING SEASON

Exodus 14:13-14 (NIV) "Moses answered the people, 'Do not be afraid. Stand firm and you will see the deliverance the Lord will bring you today. The Egyptians you see today you will never see again. The Lord will fight for you; you need only to be still.'"

Read pages 230 - 237: **DAY 31 - THE SITTING SEASON** from "40 Day Stand For Marriage Restoration."

Stand on this truth:

In Exodus 14:13-14, God instructs the Israelites to be still and trust Him to fight their battles. Similarly, as standers for marriage restoration, we enter a season of sitting, sitting in trust, knowing that God is fighting for our marriages. The sitting season may seem counterintuitive, but it's a time to release control and trust in God's power. It's about surrendering fears and anxieties and allowing God to work miracles in our marriages.

Prayer for Today:

"Heavenly Father, I surrender control to You and trust in Your plan for my marriage. Help me to be still and know that You are God, fighting for me. Grant me the strength to stand firm in faith and witness the deliverance You have promised. Thank You for Your faithfulness. In Jesus' name, I pray. Amen."

Activate Today's Lesson:

1. How does embracing the sitting season impact your stand for marriage restoration?

2. Identify and write down any lies from today's **"Lies to Reject"** that you've been struggling with. Cross them out symbolically to break their hold on your mind.

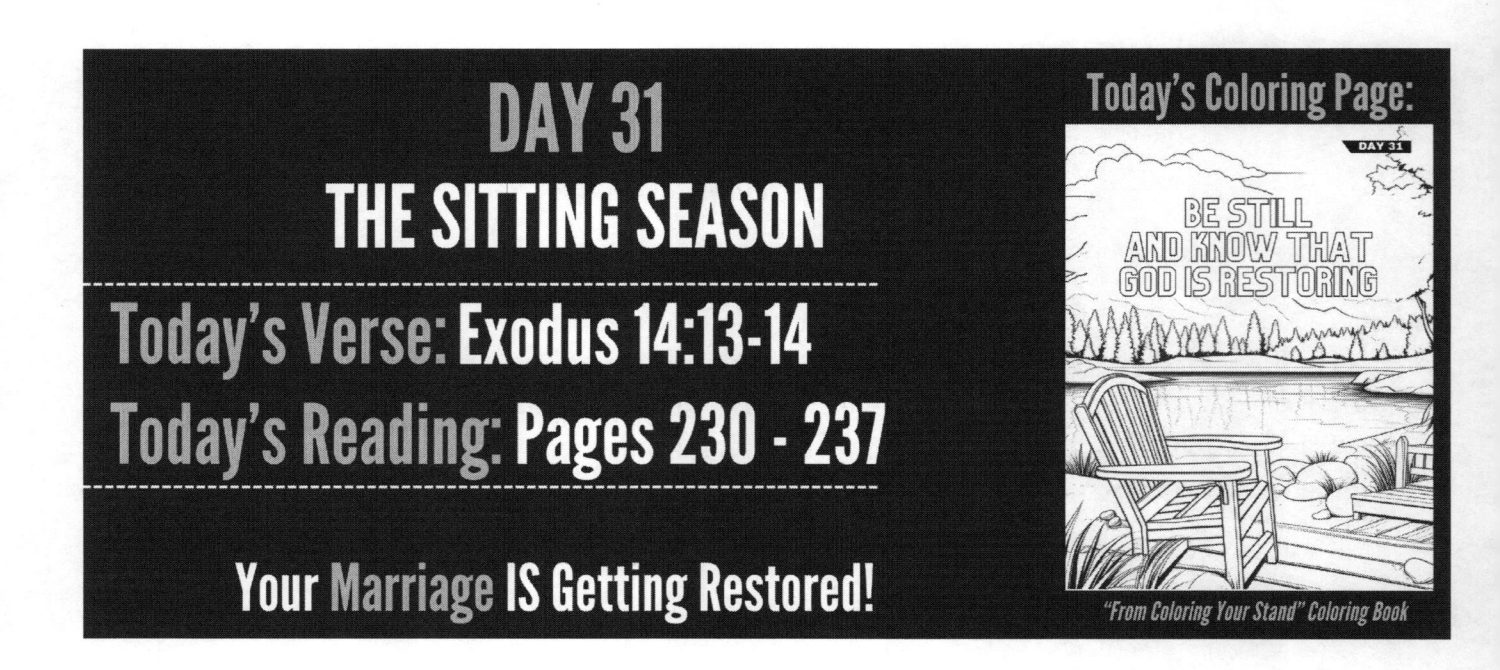

3. Write down below and begin to speak aloud a few of today's **"Daily Truths to Declare."** Believe that they are true and activated in your stand for restoration.

DAY 31
THE SITTING SEASON

Today's Verse: Exodus 14:13-14
Today's Reading: Pages 230 - 237

Your Marriage IS Getting Restored!

Today's Coloring Page:
BE STILL AND KNOW THAT GOD IS RESTORING
"From Coloring Your Stand" Coloring Book

Session 7 - Day 3

DAY 32 - JUST STAND FIRM AND DON'T GIVE UP!

Ephesians 6:13 (AMP) "Therefore put on God's complete armor, that you may be able to resist and stand your ground on the evil day [of danger], and, having done all [the crisis demands], to stand [firmly in your place]."

Read pages 238 – 245: **DAY 32 – JUST STAND FIRM AND DON'T GIVE UP!** from "40 Day Stand For Marriage Restoration."

Stand on this truth:

In Ephesians 6:13, we're reminded of the importance of putting on the complete armor of God and standing firm in the face of adversity. Sometimes, victory comes when we refuse to quit and choose to do all that the crisis demands. God calls us to be supernaturally stubborn in His promises, refusing to budge in our pursuit of restoration.

Prayer for Today:

"Heavenly Father, grant me the strength to stand firm and not give up in my stand for marriage restoration. Clothe me with Your complete armor and empower me to resist evil. Help me to persevere through the challenges and trust in Your perfect timing. I declare that I will not grow weary in doing good but will reap a harvest of restoration in due season. In Jesus' name, I pray. Amen."

Activate Today's Lesson:

1. How does embracing the concept of "Just Stand Firm and Don't Give Up" impact your stand for marriage restoration?

2. Identify and write down any lies from today's **"Lies to Reject"** that you've been struggling with. Cross them out symbolically to break their hold on your mind.

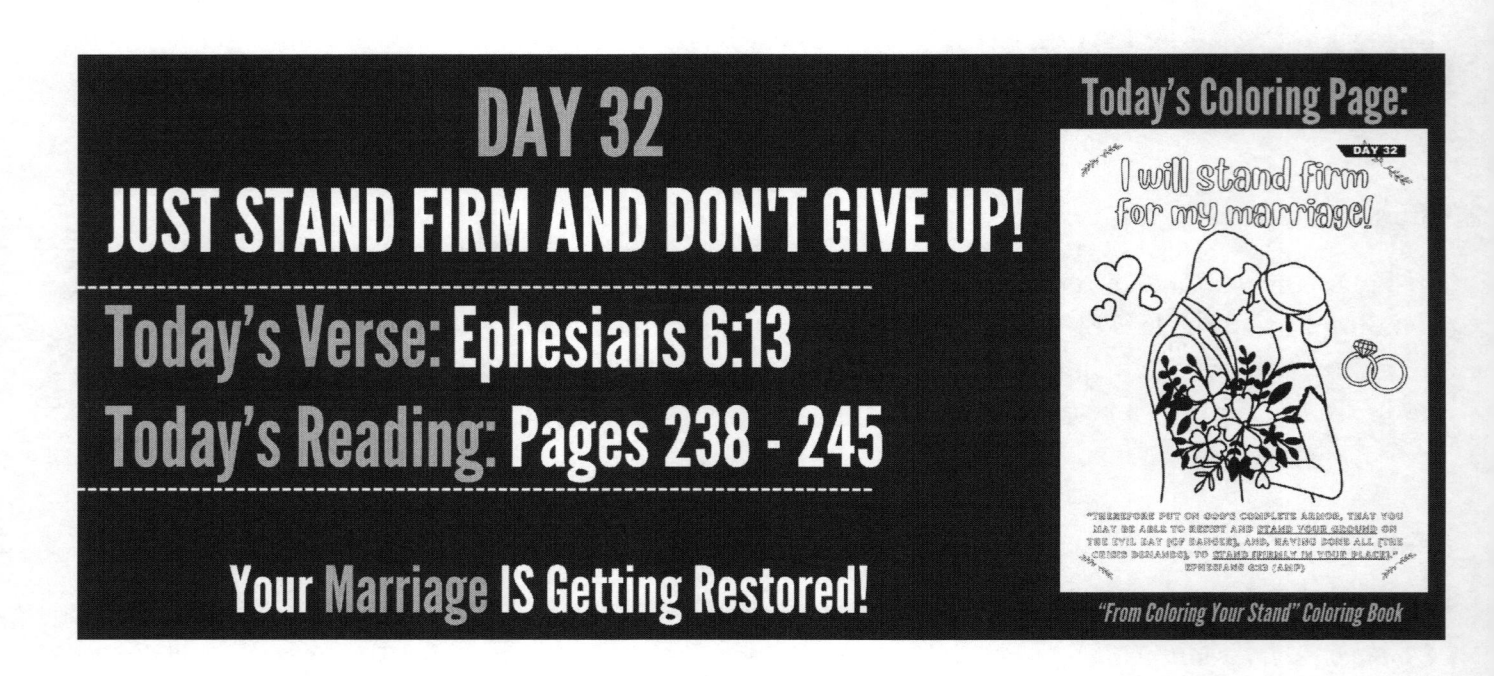

3. Write down below and begin to speak aloud a few of today's **"Daily Truths to Declare."** Believe that they are true and activated in your stand for restoration.

DAY 32

JUST STAND FIRM AND DON'T GIVE UP!

Today's Verse: Ephesians 6:13

Today's Reading: Pages 238 - 245

Your Marriage IS Getting Restored!

Today's Coloring Page:

I will stand firm for my marriage!

"THEREFORE PUT ON GOD'S COMPLETE ARMOR, THAT YOU MAY BE ABLE TO RESIST AND STAND YOUR GROUND ON THE EVIL DAY [OF DANGER], AND, HAVING DONE ALL [THE CRISIS DEMANDS], TO STAND FIRMLY IN YOUR PLACE."
EPHESIANS 6:13 (AMP)

"From Coloring Your Stand" Coloring Book

Session 7 - Day 4

Day 26 – A Wall of Fire Is Surrounding Your Spouse

Zechariah 2:5 (NASB) "'For I,' declares the Lord, 'will be a wall of fire around her, and I will be the glory in her midst.'"

Read pages 193 – 199: <u>*DAY 26 – A WALL OF FIRE IS SURROUNDING YOUR SPOUSE*</u> from "40 Day Stand For Marriage Restoration."

Stand on this truth:

Imagine and believe that a wall of fire surrounds your spouse, offering divine protection and purification. This imagery vividly portrays God's safeguarding presence, shielding your spouse from spiritual attacks and refining them from impurities.

Prayer for Today:

"Heavenly Father, thank You for the powerful promise of Zechariah 2:5. As I stand for the restoration of my spouse and marriage, I trust in Your divine protection and purification. Surround my spouse with Your wall of fire, guarding them from the enemy's schemes and refining them from within. May Your presence and glory be evident in their life, guiding them back to a place of healing and restoration. In Jesus' name, amen."

Activate Today's Lesson:

1. Consider how embracing the truth that "A Wall of Fire Is Surrounding Your Spouse" could impact your stand for marriage restoration.

2. Identify and write down any lies from today's **"Lies to Reject"** that you've been struggling with. Cross them out symbolically to break their hold on your mind.

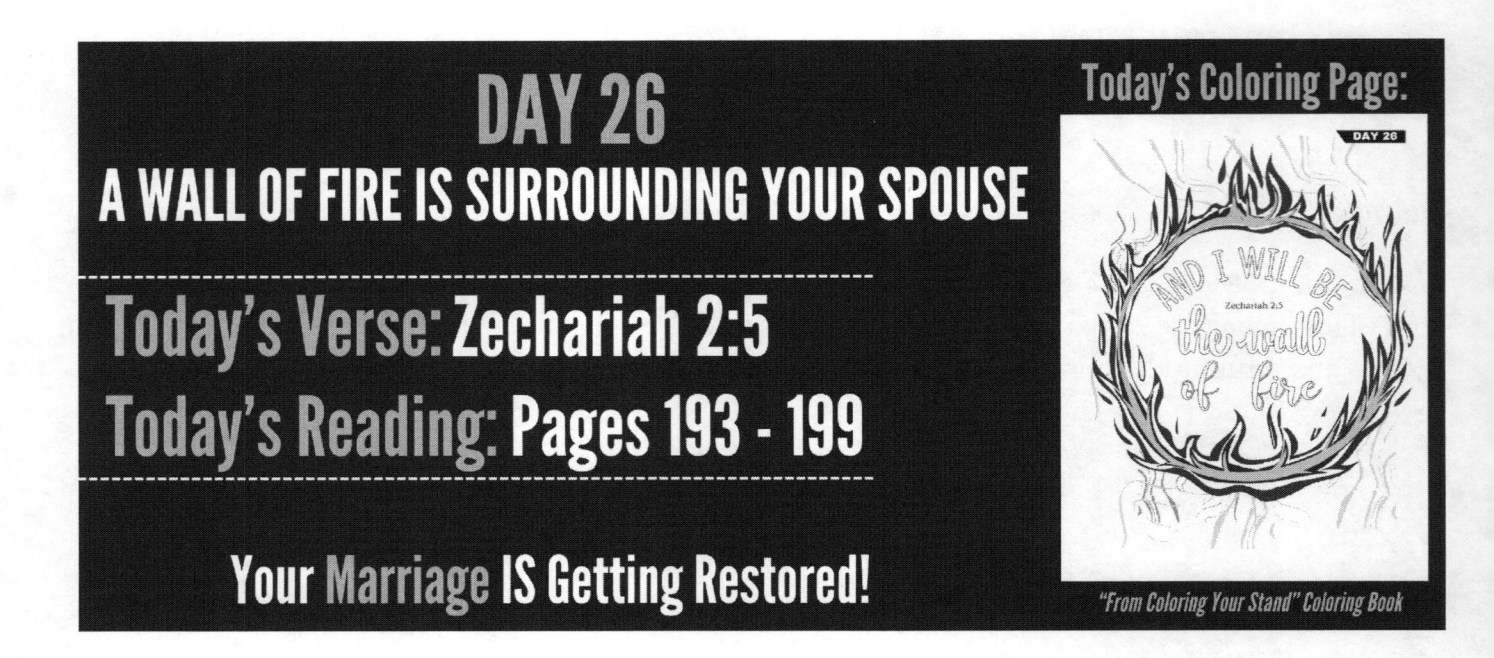

3. Write down below and begin to speak aloud a few of today's **"Daily Truths to Declare."** Believe that they are true and activated in your stand for restoration.

DAY 26
A WALL OF FIRE IS SURROUNDING YOUR SPOUSE

Today's Verse: Zechariah 2:5
Today's Reading: Pages 193 - 199

Your Marriage IS Getting Restored!

Today's Coloring Page:

"From Coloring Your Stand" Coloring Book

Session 7 - Day 5

DAY 11 – INVITE THE DIVORCE-BUSTING ANGEL TO YOUR MARRIAGE

Matthew 1:19-20 (ESV) "And her husband Joseph, being a just man and unwilling to put her to shame, resolved to divorce her quietly. But as he considered these things, behold, an angel of the Lord appeared to him in a dream, saying, 'Joseph, son of David, do not fear to take Mary as your wife, for that which is conceived in her is from the Holy Spirit.'"

Read pages 82 – 89: <u>**DAY 11 – INVITE THE DIVORCE-BUSTING ANGEL TO YOUR MARRIAGE**</u> from "40 Day Stand For Marriage Restoration."

Stand on this truth:

Just as an angel intervened to prevent Joseph from divorcing Mary, we can believe for divine intervention in our own marriages.

Prayer for Today:

"Heavenly Father, I thank You for the revelation of the angelic realm and their role in Your divine plan for marriage restoration. I invite the "divorce-busting angel" to visit my spouse with a message of reconciliation and healing. Let Your heavenly hosts actively work in our lives, leading us back together stronger than ever. In Jesus' name, amen."

Activate Today's Lesson:

1. How does the truth of Matthew 1:19-20 impact your perspective on marital restoration?

2. Identify and write down any lies from today's **"Lies to Reject"** that you've been struggling with. Cross them out symbolically to break their hold on your mind.

3. Write down below and begin to speak aloud a few of today's **"Daily Truths to Declare."** Believe that they are true and activated in your stand for restoration.

**DAY 11
INVITE THE DIVORCE-BUSTING ANGEL TO YOUR MARRIAGE**

Today's Verse: Matthew 1:19-20
Today's Reading: Pages 82 - 89

Your Marriage IS Getting Restored!

Today's Coloring Page:
"FOR HE WILL COMMAND HIS ANGELS"
"From Coloring Your Stand" Coloring Book

Session 7 - Day 6

Reviewing this week's daily readings

Spend a few moments today reviewing last week's daily readings. You will have a chance to discuss these topics at the start of next week's group session. Writing these answers ahead of time will best prepare you for next week's opening group time discussion.

What encouraging takeaways did you have from this day's reading? What specific thoughts, verses, lies, declarations, or testimonies are specifically impactful for your stand?

Day 1 – "Day 29: Stand With A Divine Perspective" insights:

Day 2 – "Day 31: The Sitting Season" insights:

Day 3 – "Day 32: Just Stand Firm And Don't Give Up!" insights:

Day 4 – "Day 26: A Wall of Fire is Surrounding Your Spouse" insights:

Day 5 – "Day 11: Invite The Divorce-Busting Angel To Your Marriage" insights:

Write this week's Memory Verse below:

Additional Notes:

SESSION 8 - STANDING IN VICTORY!

In session 8, "Standing in Victory," Pastor Jason Carver declares that you are not fighting for victory but standing from a place of victory in Christ. He explains how restoration is part of God's plan and how believers have already been equipped with everything they need to stand.
Pastor Jason encourages you to reject the lies of the enemy and live in the truth of God's promises, knowing that His love never fails. This session empowers you to embrace victory as your mindset and to walk in supernatural strength, peace, and hope as you continue your stand.

"You are not just standing for your marriage in your own strength; you have been equipped with everything you need through God's divine power. Trust in this provision and know that God has already prepared the way for your victory" – Jason Carver

Discussion and review from last week's daily readings of "40 Day Stand For Marriage Restoration."

Before you begin this week's teaching video, go around the group and discuss your insights and takeaways from each of the daily readings from last week. Revisit last week's Day 6 Workbook page for an overview of your reading takeaways.

Write any insights from other group members below:

Any specific day from last week's reading that you need to go back and read again?

Before you begin this week's Video Teaching, pray for the Holy Spirit to come and bring revelation to your stand for restoration as you watch this week's teaching.

Follow along with this week's teaching video and fill in the blanks below as the answers appear on the screen.

Session 8 — VIDEO GUIDE — STANDING FOR MARRIAGE RESTORATION

1) There is a _____ promise that God is turning the hearts of family members back to each other!

2) Your spouse's _____ is turning back to you!

3) One of the biggest lies the devil tells standers is that you _____ have what it takes and you're not going to _____ it!

4) You _____ have all the resources needed to stand for your marriage!

5) There is a guaranteed blessing just for _____ in the Lord's promises.

6) Stand on the truth that this is the season of your life when you are going to _____ in all things!

7) Love is the greatest _____ on earth.

8) Love creates _____ like nothing else can.

9) Love removes _____.

10) Love brings _____ and peace.

11) Love _____ fails!

12) It is standing in _____ _____, not your love, that will bring victory!

Discussion Questions from This Week's Teaching Video

Question #1: How does the prophetic promise in Malachi 4:5-6, which speaks of turning the hearts of family members back to each other, resonate with your stand for marriage restoration? Since Jesus said John the Baptist carried the Spirit of Elijah, can you see how this promise reveals God's will for your spouse's heart to turn back to you and your family?

Question #2: Jason mentions that one of the biggest lies the enemy tells standers is that they don't have what it takes. How can 2 Peter 1:3, which states that "His divine power has given us everything we need for life and godliness," break the lie and reinforce the truth that you already have all the resources needed to stand for your marriage? How can this impact your confidence in standing?

Question #3: In Luke 1:45, it says, "Blessed is she who has believed that what the Lord has said to her will be accomplished!" How can believing in the Lord's promises, even in the face of overwhelming odds, bring blessings into your life? Can you share examples of blessings you have experienced simply by holding onto God's promises during your stand?

Question #4: 3 John 2 mentions, "I pray that you may prosper in all things and be in health, just as your soul prospers." What do you think about this view of God wanting this season to be a time when you can prosper in all aspects of life, not just in your marriage relationship? What steps can you take to embrace this season as one of growth and prosperity in every area?

Question #5: Jason mentioned how the power of love can impact your stand. He said, "Love is the greatest motivator on earth," "Love creates perseverance like nothing else can," "Love removes fear," and "Love brings quietness and peace." Which one of these examples do you need to show up in your stand today and why?

Question #6: How might relying on Christ's love, rather than your version and ability to love, change the way you stand? Have you experienced any moments when Christ's love seemed to fill you with a deeper love and connection for your spouse? How would your stand be different if you fully relied on His love?

This Week's Memory Verse

- *2 Peter 1:3 (NIV) "His divine power has given us everything we need for life and godliness through our knowledge of him who called us by his own glory and goodness."*

- *(Bonus memory verses) - 2 Corinthians 5:14a (MSG) "Christ's love has moved me to such extremes. His love has the first and last word in everything we do…"*

This Week's Daily Readings from "40 Day Stand for Marriage Restoration"

- *Day 1: "**DAY 30 - THE PROPHETIC PROMISE OF RESTORATION**" (Pages 223 - 229)*

- *Day 2: "**DAY 33 - YOU HAVE EVERYTHING YOU NEED!**" (Pages 246 - 253)*

- *Day 3: "**DAY 37 - BLESSED FOR BELIEVING!**" (Pages 278 - 285)*

- *Day 4: "**DAY 39 - THIS IS YOUR SEASON TO PROSPER**" (Pages 293 - 300)*

- *Day 5: "**DAY 40 - IT'S NOT YOUR LOVE BUT CHRISTS'**" (Pages 301 - 307)*

Scriptures From This Week's Video Teaching

Malachi 4:5–6 (NASB) *"Behold, I am going to send you Elijah the prophet before the coming of the great and terrible day of the Lord. "And he will restore the hearts of the fathers to their children, and the hearts of the children to their fathers, lest I come and smite the land with a curse."*

Luke 1:15–17 (NASB) *"For he will be great in the sight of the Lord, and he will drink no wine or liquor; and he will be filled with the Holy Spirit, while yet in his mother's womb. "And he will turn back many of the sons of Israel to the Lord their God. "And it is he who will go as a forerunner before Him in the spirit and power of Elijah, to turn the hearts of the fathers back to the children, and the disobedient to the attitude of the righteous; so as to make ready a people prepared for the Lord."*

Matthew 11:14 (AMP) *"And if you are willing to receive and accept it, John himself is Elijah who was to come [before the kingdom]."*

2 Corinthians 5:18 (ESV) *"All this is from God, who reconciled us to himself through Christ and gave us the ministry of reconciliation."*

Ezekiel 11:19 ((NIV) *"I will give them an undivided heart and put a new spirit in them; I will remove from them their heart of stone and give them a heart of flesh."*

Deuteronomy 30:6 ((NIV) *"The Lord your God will circumcise your hearts and the hearts of your descendants, so that you may love him with all your heart and with all your soul, and live."*

Jeremiah 24:7 (NIV) "I will give them a heart to know me, that I am the Lord. They will be my people, and I will be their God, for they will return to me with all their heart."

2 Peter 1:3 (NIV) "His divine power has given us everything we need for life and godliness through our knowledge of him who called us by his own glory and goodness."

John 3:34 (ESV) "For he whom God has sent utters the words of God, for he gives the Spirit without measure."

Ephesians 1:3 (ESV) "Blessed be the God and Father of our Lord Jesus Christ, who <u>has</u> blessed us in Christ with every spiritual blessing in the heavenly places,"

Luke 1:45 (NIV) "Blessed is she who has believed that what the Lord has said to her will be accomplished!"

John 11:40 (NKJV) "Did I not say to you that if you would believe you would see the glory of God?"

Psalm 84:11 (NIV) "For the Lord God is a sun and shield; the Lord bestows favor and honor; no good thing does he withhold from those whose walk is blameless."

Ephesians 1:3 (NIV) "Praise be to the God and Father of our Lord Jesus Christ, who has blessed us in the heavenly realms with every spiritual blessing in Christ."

3 John 2 (NKJV) "Beloved, I pray that you may prosper in all things and be in health, just as your soul prospers"

Psalm 1:3 (NIV) "That person is like a tree planted by streams of water, which yields its fruit in season and whose leaf does not wither—whatever they do prospers."

Jeremiah 29:11 (NIV) "For I know the plans I have for you, declares the Lord, plans for welfare and not for evil, to give you a future and a hope."

Psalm 34:10 (NIV) "The lions may grow weak and hungry, but those who seek the Lord lack no good thing."

Proverbs 10:22 (NIV) "The blessing of the Lord brings wealth, without painful toil for it."

2 Corinthians 5:14a (ESV) "For the love of Christ controls us,… because we have concluded this: that one has died for all, therefore all have died;"

2 Corinthians 5:14a (TPT) "For it is Christ's love that fuels our passion and motivates us, …."

2 Corinthians 5:14a (MSG) "Christ's love has moved me to such extremes. His love has the first and last word in everything we do…"

1 Corinthians 13:4 (ESV) "Love is patient"

1 Corinthians 13:7 (ESV) "Love bears all things, believes all things, hopes all things, endures all things."

Genesis 29:20 (ESV) "So Jacob served seven years for Rachel, and they seemed to him but a few days because of the love he had for her."

1 John 4:18 (ESV) *"There is no fear in love, but perfect love casts out fear. For fear has to do with punishment, and whoever fears has not been perfected in love."*

Zephaniah 3:17 (ESV) *"The LORD your God is in your midst, a mighty one who will save; he will rejoice over you with gladness; he will quiet you by his love; he will exult over you with loud singing."*

1 Corinthians 13:8 (NIV) *"Love never fails. But where there are prophecies, they will cease; where there are tongues, they will be stilled; where there is knowledge, it will pass away."*

SESSION 8 - DAY 1

DAY 30: THE PROPHETIC PROMISE OF RESTORATION!

Malachi 4:5-6 (NASB) "Behold, I am going to send you Elijah the prophet... He will turn the hearts of the fathers back to their children, and the hearts of the children back to their fathers..."

Read pages 223 - 229: *Day 30: The Prophetic Promise of Restoration!* from "40 Day Stand For Marriage Restoration."

Stand on this truth:

In Malachi 4:5-6, God promises to send Elijah the prophet, who will turn the hearts of family members back to each other. This promise extends beyond ancient times and speaks directly to the desire for restoration and reconciliation in our marriages. God's promise of restoration through Elijah signifies His desire to reconcile broken relationships and heal wounded hearts. Just as John the Baptist prepared hearts for Jesus, God is preparing and softening the hearts of spouses for marital restoration.

Prayer for Today:

"Heavenly Father, I believe in Your promise of restoration for my marriage. Just as You turned the hearts of fathers and children, I trust You to turn my spouse's heart back to me. Work in us both, softening our hearts and drawing us closer together. I surrender my doubts and fears, knowing that Your desire is for restoration. In Jesus' name, I pray. Amen."

Activate Today's Lesson:

1. How does embracing the prophetic promise of restoration impact your stand for marriage restoration?

2. Identify and write down any lies from today's **"Lies to Reject"** that you've been struggling with. Cross them out symbolically to break their hold on your mind.

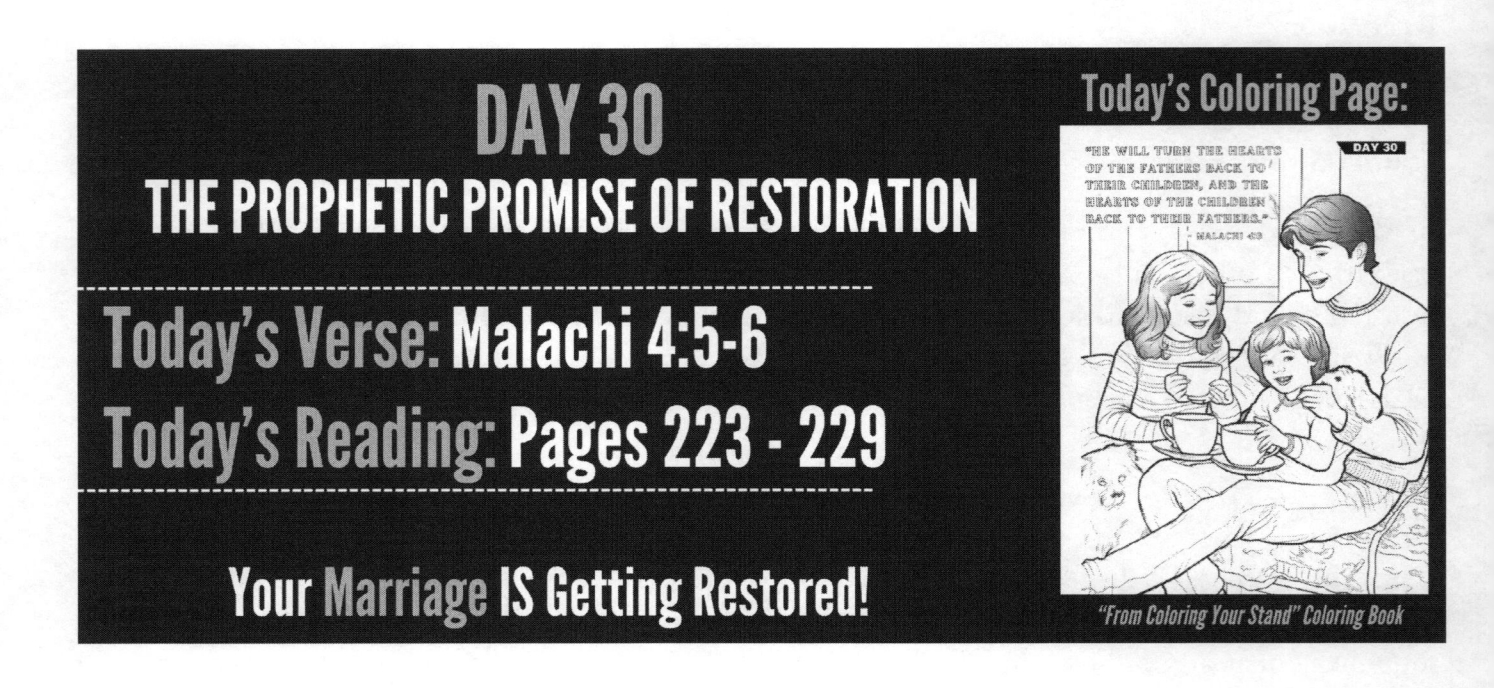

3. Write down below and begin to speak aloud a few of today's **"Daily Truths to Declare."** Believe that they are true and activated in your stand for restoration.

DAY 30
THE PROPHETIC PROMISE OF RESTORATION

Today's Verse: Malachi 4:5-6
Today's Reading: Pages 223 - 229

Your Marriage IS Getting Restored!

Today's Coloring Page:

"HE WILL TURN THE HEARTS OF THE FATHERS BACK TO THEIR CHILDREN, AND THE HEARTS OF THE CHILDREN BACK TO THEIR FATHERS."
— MALACHI 4:9

"From Coloring Your Stand" Coloring Book

Session 8 - Day 2

Day 33: You Have Everything You Need!

2 Peter 1:3 (NIV) "His divine power has given us everything we need for life and godliness through our knowledge of him who called us by his own glory and goodness."

Read pages 246 - 253: *Day 33: You Have Everything You Need!* from "40 Day Stand For Marriage Restoration."

Stand on this truth:

In 2 Peter 1:3, we're reminded that God's divine power has already provided us with everything we need for life and godliness. Despite feeling unequipped or lacking resources, God has equipped us with all we need for this journey. Feeling ill-equipped or lacking resources is common when standing for marriage restoration. However, the truth is that God has already provided everything we need for this journey.

Prayer for Today:

"Heavenly Father, thank you for equipping me with everything I need for the restoration of my marriage. Strengthen my faith and grant me wisdom to access your abundant provisions. Help me trust in your perfect timing and believe in the supernatural resources you have provided. I declare that I am empowered for this journey and will witness your glory in the restoration of my marriage. In Jesus' name, I pray. Amen."

Activate Today's Lesson:

1. How does embracing the truth that you have everything you need impact your stand for marriage restoration?

2. Identify and write down any lies from today's **"Lies to Reject"** that you've been struggling with. Cross them out symbolically to break their hold on your mind.

3. Write down below and begin to speak aloud a few of today's **"Daily Truths to Declare."** Believe that they are true and activated in your stand for restoration.

DAY 33
YOU HAVE EVERYTHING YOU NEED!

Today's Verse: 2 Peter 1:3
Today's Reading: Pages 246 - 253

Your Marriage IS Getting Restored!

Today's Coloring Page:

"From Coloring Your Stand" Coloring Book

Session 8 - Day 3

Day 37: Blessed For Believing!

Luke 1:45 (NIV) "Blessed is she who has believed that what the Lord has said to her will be accomplished!"

Read pages 278 – 285: *__Day 37: Blessed For Believing!__* from "40 Day Stand For Marriage Restoration."

Stand on this truth:

Believing in the promise of restoration requires unwavering faith and trust in God's word. It's essential to recognize that as you stand in faith, God desires to bless you abundantly. Just as Mary was blessed for her unwavering belief in God's promise, so too are you blessed as you trust in His promise of restoration for your marriage.

Prayer for Today:

"Heavenly Father, I thank You for the blessings You have bestowed upon me as I believe in the restoration of my marriage. Help me to maintain unwavering faith and trust in Your promises. May Your blessings overflow in every area of my life, and may Your glory be revealed through the restoration of my marriage. In Jesus' name, amen."

Activate Today's Lesson:

1. How have you seen the blessings of God manifesting in your life as you stand for marital restoration?

2. Identify and write down any lies from today's **"Lies to Reject"** that you've been struggling with. Cross them out symbolically to break their hold on your mind.

3. Write down below and begin to speak aloud a few of today's **"Daily Truths to Declare."** Believe that they are true and activated in your stand for restoration.

DAY 37
BLESSED FOR BELIEVING!

Today's Verse: Luke 1:45
Today's Reading: Pages 278 - 285

Your Marriage IS Getting Restored!

Today's Coloring Page:

"From Coloring Your Stand" Coloring Book

Session 8 - Day 4

Day 39: This Is Your Season to Prosper!

3 John 2 (NKJV) "Beloved, I pray that you may prosper in all things and be in good health, just as your soul prospers."

Read pages 293 - 300: *Day 39: This Is Your Season to Prosper!* from "40 Day Stand For Marriage Restoration."

Stand on this truth:

During this season of standing for marriage restoration, it's easy to focus on the challenges and pain, overlooking the potential for prosperity in all areas of life. However, this verse reminds us of God's desire for our holistic well-being and prosperity.

Prayer for Today:

"Heavenly Father, thank You for Your promise of prosperity in all things. I declare that, as I stand for the restoration of my marriage, I will experience Your blessings in my health, finances, soul, and all areas of my life. Help me to trust in Your provision and plan for my life. In Jesus' name, amen."

Activate Today's Lesson:

1. How could embracing the truth that this is your season to prosper impact your stand for marriage restoration?

2. Identify and write down any lies from today's **"Lies to Reject"** that you've been struggling with. Cross them out symbolically to break their hold on your mind.

3. Write down below and begin to speak aloud a few of today's **"Daily Truths to Declare."** Believe that they are true and activated in your stand for restoration.

DAY 39

THIS IS YOUR SEASON TO PROSPER

Today's Verse: **3 John 2**

Today's Reading: **Pages 293 - 300**

Your Marriage IS Getting Restored!

Today's Coloring Page:

"BELOVED, I PRAY THAT YOU MAY PROSPER IN ALL THINGS AND BE IN HEALTH, JUST AS YOUR SOUL PROSPERS"
3 JOHN 1:2

"From Coloring Your Stand" Coloring Book

SESSION 8 - DAY 5

DAY 40: IT'S NOT YOUR LOVE BUT CHRIST'S!

2 Corinthians 5:14 (TPT) "For it is Christ's love that fuels our passion and motivates us, because we are absolutely convinced that he has given his life for all of us. This means all died with him."

Read pages 301 - 307: **Day 40: It's Not Your Love but Christ's!** from "40 Day Stand For Marriage Restoration."

Stand on this truth:

As we conclude our 40-day journey, it's crucial to embrace the truth that it's not our love alone that sustains us through the challenges of standing for marriage restoration. Rather, it's the boundless love of Christ that empowers and motivates us to persevere.

Prayer for Today:

"Heavenly Father, thank You for the revelation that it's not my love but the boundless love of Christ that empowers me to stand for the restoration of my marriage. Fill me with Your love, grace, and compassion, enabling me to love in the strength of Jesus. In Jesus' name, amen."

Activate Today's Lesson:

1. Reflect on how embracing the truth that it's not your love but Christ's love can impact your stand for marriage restoration.

2. Identify and write down any lies from today's **"Lies to Reject"** that you've been struggling with. Cross them out symbolically to break their hold on your mind.

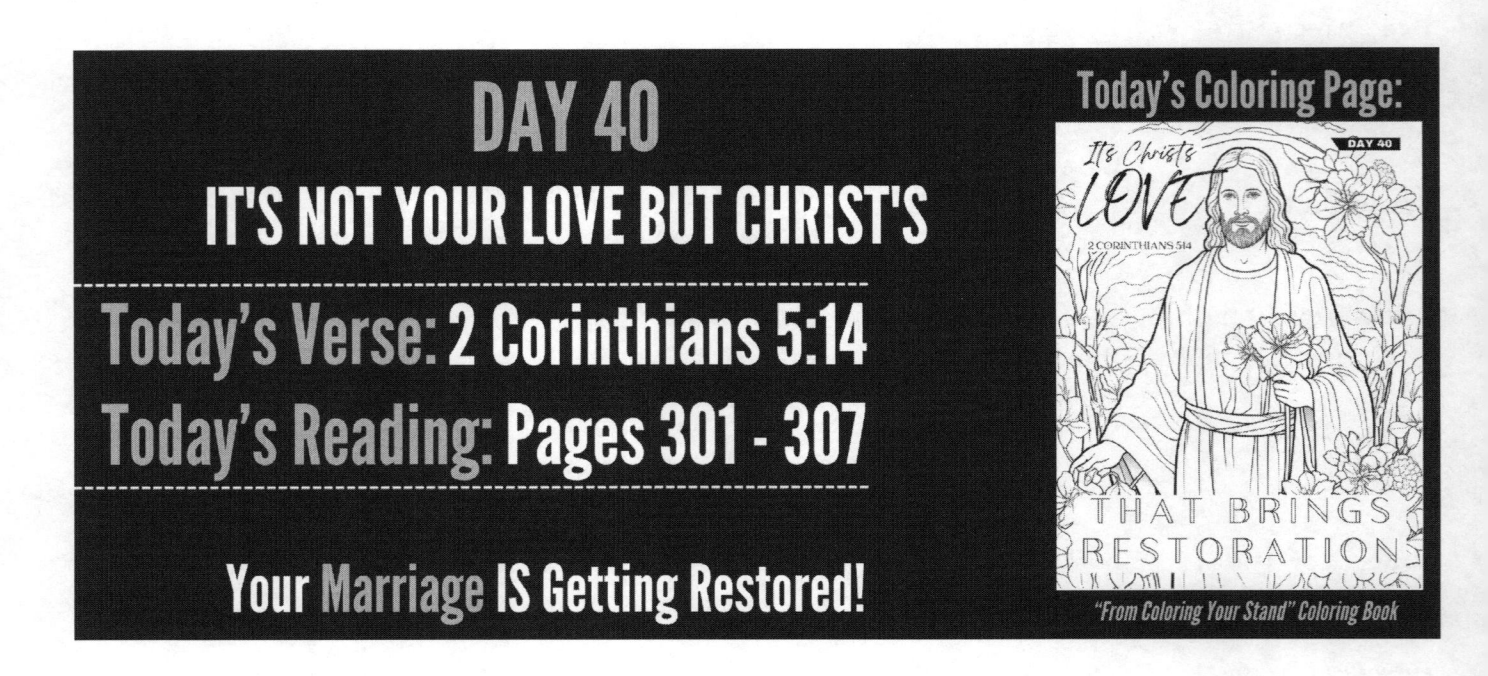

3. Write down below and begin to speak aloud a few of today's **"Daily Truths to Declare."** Believe that they are true and activated in your stand for restoration.

DAY 40
IT'S NOT YOUR LOVE BUT CHRIST'S

Today's Verse: 2 Corinthians 5:14
Today's Reading: Pages 301 - 307

Your Marriage IS Getting Restored!

Today's Coloring Page:
"From Coloring Your Stand" Coloring Book

SESSION 8 - DAY 6

REVIEWING THIS WEEK'S DAILY READINGS

Spend a few moments today reviewing last week's daily readings. You will have a chance to discuss these topics at the start of next week's group session. Writing these answers ahead of time will best prepare you for next week's opening group time discussion.

What encouraging takeaways did you have from this day's reading? What specific thoughts, verses, lies, declarations, or testimonies are specifically impactful for your stand?

Day 1 – "*Day 30: The Prophetic Promise of Restoration*" insights:

Day 2 – "*Day 33: You Have Everything You Need!*" insights:

Day 3 – "*Day 37: Blessed For Believing!* " insights:

Day 4 – "*Day 39: This Is Your Season To Prosper*" insights:

Day 5 – "*Day 40: It's Not Your Love But Christ's!*" insights:

Write this week's Memory Verse below:

Additional Notes:

SESSION 9 - A SPOUSE'S PERSPECTIVE

In this final session, "A Spouse's Perspective," Pastor Jason Carver is joined by his wife, Christine, who shares her powerful testimony of how God transformed her heart during their separation. Christine offers honest insights into the lies, struggles, and spiritual battles she faced and how God's love ultimately brought her to repentance and reconciliation. Her story provides encouragement for participants to persevere in faith, trust in God's timing, and believe that He is working behind the scenes to soften hearts and restore marriages. This session is a powerful reminder that no situation is beyond God's ability to redeem and heal.

"You have the power to carry hope for your marriage, even if your spouse has lost hope. I really want to encourage you to stand on Psalm 71:14, which says, 'As for me, I will always have hope. I will praise you more and more.' No matter what people are saying around you, you can still have hope." – Christine Carver

Discussion and Review from last week's daily readings of "40 Day Stand For Marriage Restoration."

Before you begin this week's teaching video, go around the group and discuss your insights and takeaways from each of the daily readings from last week. Revisit last week's Day 6 Workbook page for an overview of your reading takeaways.

Write any insights from other group members below:

Any specific day from last week's reading that you need to go back and read again?

Before you begin this week's Video Teaching, pray for the Holy Spirit to come and bring revelation to your stand for restoration as you watch this week's teaching.

Follow along with this week's teaching video and fill in the blanks below as the answers appear on the screen.

Session 9 — VIDEO GUIDE
STANDING FOR MARRIAGE RESTORATION

1) You have the power to carry _____ for your marriage, even if your spouse has lost hope.

2) The enemy is the greatest _____ ever! He presents himself in a way that appears good and harmless, making it easy for your spouse to fall into his traps.

3) You have the power to _____ and have your spouse's eyes _____ so they can see!

4) Don't be shocked if you hear your spouse _____ somebody said it's ok to leave, or that it's _____ they are moving on.

5) God _____ _____ given up on your spouse; He is still pursuing them even if your spouse may not be _____ God.

6) God's love and kindness, not _____, is what brings change and healing to your spouse.

7) Your faith can _____ what your spouse's eyes cannot.

8) Never lose hope that God can change hearts _____ and unexpectedly. What seems impossible one day can become a _____ the very next day!

9) If we are _____ much, the Bible says that we _____ much.

10) Never forget, God is able to do far _____ than you can even dream and _____.

Discussion Questions from This Week's Teaching Video

Question #1: What part of Christine's talk resonated most with you, and why?

Question #2: Christine mentioned how important it was that Jason carried hope for their marriage, even when she had lost hope. How challenging has it been for you to remain hopeful when your spouse has lost hope? What steps can you take to increase your hope during this time?

Question #3: Christine shared how easy it was for her, and likely your own spouse, to be deceived by the enemy. What do you think about her statement that "You have the power to pray and have your spouse's eyes opened so they can see"? Does hearing Christine's testimony of how her eyes were radically opened encourage you in your own stand?

Question #4: Christine mentioned that during her time away, she believed it was okay to move on, influenced by advice from pastors and counselors. How do you prepare yourself for the possibility of your spouse saying that someone advised them it's okay to leave or move on? How can you continue to stand in faith and hope without being shocked or discouraged by these statements?

Question #5: Jason and Christine's story reminds us that we can see in faith what our spouse's eyes cannot. What are some ways you have learned through this study to increase your faith so you can see possibilities for restoration that your spouse may not currently see?

Question #6: Christine's return home was sudden and unexpected. How does Ephesians 3:20 encourage you that this could also happen for you and your spouse? How does believing that God can do far more than you can dream or imagine shape the way you pray and stand for your spouse's heart to change?

Question #7: Christine shared how the forgiveness she has felt from the Lord and from Jason has transformed her heart. She shared how the Bible says, "If we are forgiven much, we love much" (paraphrase of Luke 7:47). Spend a few moments as a group praying for each other spouses to feel such love and forgiveness that they can't help but overflow with a greater love for the Lord and for your family.

Spend some time praying for each other and praying for each other's spouse by name. Also be sure to revisit the "Honoring Our Stand and Spouse - Standing Class Contract" from the beginning of the workbook and make sure you have everybody's name written down so you continue to pray for them after the study is completed.

Scriptures From This Week's Video Teaching

Psalm 71:14 (NIV) "As for me, I will always have hope; I will praise you more and more."

2 Corinthians 11:14 (NASB) "No wonder, for even Satan disguises himself as an angel of light."

2 Corinthians 4:4 (NIV) "The god of this age has blinded the minds of unbelievers, so that they cannot see the light of the gospel that displays the glory of Christ, who is the image of God."

Isaiah 65:1 (NIV) "I revealed myself to those who did not ask for me; I was found by those who did not seek me. To a nation that did not call on my name, I said, 'Here am I, here am I.'"

Romans 2:4 (NASB) "Or do you think lightly of the riches of His kindness and tolerance and patience, not knowing that the kindness of God leads you to repentance?" "

Hebrews 11:1 (NASB) "Now faith is the assurance of things hoped for, the conviction of things not seen."

Proverbs 21:1 (NASB) "The king's heart is like channels of water in the hand of the Lord; He turns it wherever He pleases."

Luke 7:47 (NKJV) "Therefore I say to you, her sins, which are many, are forgiven, for she loved much. But to whom little is forgiven, the same loves little."

Ephesians 3:20 (NASB) "Now to Him who is able to do far more abundantly beyond all that we ask or think, according to the power that works within us."

Conclusion: What's Next?

Conclusion: What's Next?

Congratulations on completing the "Standing for Marriage Restoration" workbook! You've taken a significant and faith-filled step toward the restoration of your marriage, and I want to commend you for your dedication and perseverance. This journey has been about more than just waiting for change; it's been about deepening your relationship with God, trusting in His promises, and allowing Him to transform your heart as you stand in faith.

As you move forward, I encourage you to keep seeking God daily through prayer, His Word, and the guidance of the Holy Spirit. Remember that God is always working, even when you can't see it, and He is faithful to bring about the restoration He has promised. Your marriage, no matter how hopeless it may seem, is not beyond God's ability to heal and restore.

But your journey doesn't end here, there are exciting ways to continue growing, learning, and standing supernaturally for your marriage. Here's how you can stay connected and deepen your stand:

Join Our Monthly Membership Program

We invite you to continue this journey with us by becoming a part of our one-of-a-kind monthly membership program. This program offers special resources and support for those standing for marriage restoration that you won't find anywhere else. You'll gain access to exclusive teachings, encouragement, and a community of standers who understand what you're going through. Sign up today for a **FREE 30-day trial** and see how this program can help you stand strong in your faith. Visit www.StandingSupernaturally.com/Membership to learn more.

Take Your Stand to the Next Level: The Standing Supernaturally Academy

If you're ready to take your stand to a deeper level, I strongly encourage you to sign up for the Standing Supernaturally Academy. This groundbreaking 13-week eCourse is specifically designed to equip you with the tools, knowledge, and spiritual strength to stand supernaturally for your marriage. This Academy is NOT just this book; it has over 80 videos and over 20 hours of teaching from Jason on standing for your marriage. We only offer this program a couple of times a year, so be sure to sign up for the waiting list to be notified when registration opens. Don't miss out on this opportunity to transform your stand. Visit www.StandingSupernaturally.com/Academy to join the waiting list.

Get One-on-One Counseling from Jason

For more personalized guidance, you can schedule a 1-on-1 counseling session with Jason, where he can speak directly into your stand and situation. It's an opportunity to get specific advice and support tailored to your unique circumstances. Jason is a Board Certified Christian Counselor with two decades of pastoral staff experience. For more information, visit www.StandingSupernaturally.com/Counseling

Other Free Standing Supernaturally Resources!

We offer a variety of free resources to support you in your stand. Take our **Standing Assessment Quiz** to see how well you're currently standing and where you can improve. Visit www.StandingSupernaturally.com/Assessment to take the simple 20-question assessment.

You can also access our **Training Hub Media Site**, which is packed with free sermons, teachings, and other resources to help you grow in your faith. Create a free account and access all these resources at https://Training.StandingSupernaturally.com/

I know this journey is challenging, but remember, you are not alone. We are here to walk alongside you, offering support, encouragement, and resources as you continue to stand supernaturally for your marriage. Never forget that God is faithful. He honors your commitment and your stand. As you continue to trust Him and seek His guidance, I want you to have confidence that He is working all things together for your good and for the restoration of your marriage. Keep believing, keep praying, and keep standing supernaturally—because with God, all things are possible.

Thank you for allowing us to be part of your journey. May God continue to strengthen you, guide you, and bring His supernatural restoration to your marriage.

Jason & Christine Carver

Standing Supernaturally Ministries

Visit us at: www.StandingSupernaturally.com

APPENDIX: STANDING AT A DISTANCE WHEN NECESSARY

STANDING AT A DISTANCE WHEN NECESSARY

There are times when standing for your marriage requires you to take a step back—literally. If you are in an unsafe environment, particularly one involving domestic abuse, it is crucial to prioritize your safety and the safety of any children involved. God cares deeply about your well-being and does not expect you to remain in harm's way as you wait for your spouse to be healed and your marriage to be restored.

Understanding the Need for Safety

Standing for your marriage does not mean subjecting yourself to abuse. While God has the power to heal every broken aspect of your spouse's heart and mind, He also values your safety. The Bible teaches us that we are fearfully and wonderfully made, and our bodies are temples of the Holy Spirit (Psalm 139:14, 1 Corinthians 6:19). Therefore, it is essential to protect yourself from harm while believing in God's intervention.

If you are in a situation where your spouse is physically, emotionally, or verbally abusive, it is imperative to create a healthy distance. This distance is not an act of giving up; rather, it is a necessary step in trusting God to work on your spouse's heart from afar while you remain in a safe place. The Lord calls us to peace (1 Corinthians 7:15), and sometimes, peace means stepping away from a dangerous situation.

Encouragement to Stand Safely

We absolutely believe in God's ability to heal and transform even the most broken and dysfunctional relationships. There is nothing too hard for the Lord, and His power to redeem and restore is limitless. However, standing for your marriage from a safe place does not diminish your faith; in fact, it strengthens it. By taking necessary steps to protect yourself, you are trusting God to work in your spouse's life while you maintain your own safety and well-being. Many men and women have found themselves in similar situations, where they had to create distance between themselves and their spouses due to abusive behaviors. These actions do not negate their stand for their marriage but rather demonstrate wisdom and discernment.

We have a wonderful testimony in the book "40 Day Stand" of a marriage that experienced domestic abuse. Through counseling, faith, and the healing power of God, the abusive behavior was healed, and the couple is now in a healthy, loving marriage. This testimony is a reminder that God can heal abusers and redeem all things sinful and broken. However, we cannot stress enough that it is crucial to stand for your spouse's healing from a safe space.

Practical Steps for Those in Unsafe Situations

1. Get to a safe place: If you are in a domestic abuse situation, we urge you to seek safety immediately. This may involve staying with a trusted friend or family member or going to a shelter. Your physical and emotional safety is paramount.

2. Seek support: Surround yourself with a support system that understands your situation and can provide the help you need. This may include friends, family, church leaders, or professional counselors.

3. Pray for your spouse from a distance: Continue to intercede for your spouse's healing and deliverance, but do so from a place of safety. Pray for God to soften their heart, break the chains of abusive behavior, and bring true transformation to their life.

4. Trust God's timing: Understand that healing and restoration may take time. Trust in God's perfect timing and continue to stand in faith, knowing that He is working, even when you cannot see immediate changes.

5. Stay encouraged: Remember that God is with you every step of the way. He sees your pain, He knows your heart, and He is actively working on your behalf. You are not alone in this journey.

Important Resources

If you are in a domestic abuse situation, please seek help immediately. You can contact the National Domestic Violence Hotline at **1-800-799-7233** for confidential support and resources. Your safety is a priority, and there are people ready to help you.

Final Thoughts on Standing at a Distance Safely

Standing for your marriage is a courageous and faith-filled supernatural journey, but it's vitally important to remember that your safety should never be compromised in the process. God's heart is for your protection just as much as it is for the healing of your spouse. Sometimes, the path to restoration requires that you create physical distance, not as a sign of giving up, but as a necessary step of wisdom and trust in God's timing and power.

Believe that God is more than capable of restoring your marriage, even while you stand from a place of safety. He is faithful and sees your heart. As you continue to seek Him and trust in His plan, know that He will honor your stand.

I want you to find peace and strength in knowing that God is with you, shielding you and working behind the scenes to bring everything together for good, even when you're at a distance. Let the testimony of God's miraculous healing in the face of abuse fill you with hope and courage because, with God, absolutely nothing is impossible.

Standing Supernaturally with You,

Jason & Christine Carver

Appendix: Video Guide - Answers

Session 1 - Foundations of Standing Supernaturally for Your Marriage

1) God IS Restoring Marriages even **AFTER** Separation or Divorce.

2) Standing for your marriage isn't **IGNORING** the current reality of your marriage, but rather trusting in God's **POWER** to heal ALL the current brokenness in your marriage.

3) It's time we change the paradigm of how we think and talk about marriages from marriages constantly being in trouble, to something God is actively blessing, protecting, and even **RESURRECTING**!

4) "You plus God makes the **MAJORITY**" - John Knox

5) We must never forget that **RESTORATION** & **RESURRECTION** are at the core of the gospel! They are the very foundation of our faith.

6) The devil is actively trying to convince you that your **SPECIFIC** situation is more difficult than most and is probably too hard to be restored!

7) Make it your goal during this study to get to know and encounter the **GOD** of **HOPE**!

Session 2 - Spiritual Warfare Over Marriages

1) Marriage is a **PROPHETIC** picture of Jesus and His love for the church. By attacking marriages, the devil aims to attack Jesus. The devil can't destroy Jesus, so he is trying to destroy what Jesus LOVES.

2) There is a **SPIRITUAL** war going on over your marriage!

3) Your marriage battle is not against your **SPOUSE** but against the **SPIRITUAL** forces coming against you both.

4) If you are going to stand for your marriage you must become FAMILIAR with and no longer oblivious to the **WAYS** of the **DEVIL**.

5) The enemy is actively trying to **BLIND** the **MINDS** of our spouses so they no longer **BELIEVE** and can't **SEE** anything good in the marriage.

6) Jesus' mission was to **DESTROY** all the works of the devil, and that includes the devil's work against your **MARRIAGE**.

7) **YOU** have been authorized by Jesus to trample on the demonic influences against your marriage and **OVERCOME** all the power of the enemy.

Session 3 – Reconciliation and Repentance

1) **YOU** have been ordained by God to be a **MINISTER** of **RECONCILIATION** to the people around you!

2) As a minister of reconciliation, you must learn to not count your spouse's **SINS** against them.

3) Repentance starts with **ME**!

4) Repentance opens the door for times of **REFRESHING** to come into your life!

5) Yes, **REPENTANCE** is needed for the restoration of your marriage to occur but most people are **UNAWARE** of how to **BIBLICALLY** partner with God to help others repent.

6) I never want to be on the same side as the **DEVIL**. I will not pray for things the devil is wanting my spouse to experience!

7) While God's discipline is a reality and can lead to repentance, it is **GOD** who decides the form and timing of such discipline, **NOT** us.

8) If you are desiring your spouse to go through hardships, you should probably examine the levels of **HURT**, **BITTERNESS**, and **UNFORGIVENESS** that are still present in your heart.

9) Do not be afraid of God showing your spouse **KINDNESS**! Reject the lie that God's kindness means He **APPROVES** of their actions.

10) God's **KINDNESS** is the biblical agent that brings forth repentance!

11) Pray God gives **BOTH** you and your spouse the **GIFT** of being able to repent!

Session 4 – Standing With A Healed Heart: Grief, Shame, Fear, and Forgiveness

1) Grieving the death of your marriage doesn't mean you lack **FAITH** for the resurrection; it just means you are processing your emotions **HEALTHILY**.

2) God **BLESSES** you when you mourn in His presence!

3) Don't ever be **ASHAMED** for standing for your marriage.

4) The enemy will use **FEAR** to cripple your heart as you stand for restoration.

5) When you sense fear rising in your heart ask God to give you more **POWER**, more **LOVE**, and His **SOUND MIND**.

6) Every time fear rises in your heart, ask for **PERFECT LOVE** to come and drive it out!

7) Forgiveness is your part, whether they respond or not, whether they ask for it or not, whether they even recognize they need it or not. You forgive for **YOUR** sake.

8) Begin by praying for the strength to forgive. It may be a **GRADUAL** process, but it's crucial for your healing and restoration.

Session 5 - The Promise, Price, and Power of Hope

1) "**BIBLICAL** hope is a **CONFIDENT EXPECTATION** and trust in God's promises while providing strength and **PERSEVERANCE** during trials, that fill us with **JOY** and peace through the Holy Spirit."

2) The Spiritual battle coming against you is an attack on your **HOPE**.

3) There is a sustaining element in having **JOY** attached to hope.

4) God promises that you will experience His **GOODNESS** when your hope is truly in Him.

5) Hope always has an element of **PATIENCE**.

6) Hope-filled faith is tested in the **WAITING.**

7) Some things will only be won through **ENDURANCE** and **LONG-SUFFERING.**

8) **THE STOCKDALE PARADOX:** "You must never confuse faith that you will **PREVAIL** in the end—which you can never afford to lose—with the discipline to confront the most brutal facts of your **CURRENT** reality, whatever they might be." - *Admiral Jim Stockdale*

7) "Hope was the most **POWERFUL** thing I had when standing for my marriage. Hope was the **LIFELINE** that kept me going when everything else seemed lost." - *Jason Carver*

8) "Hope is being able to **SEE** that there is light **DESPITE** all of the darkness." - *Quote from Desmond Tutu*

Session 6 - Standing Aware of the Enemy's Plans

1) We must become **AWARE** of the devil's schemes to undermine our stand for restoration.

2) Our weapons are not of **HUMAN** effort but come from God's supernatural spiritual armory.

3) God has given **YOU** divine power to break down the **STRONGHOLDS** standing against your marriage.

4) Don't let the enemy lure you into fighting with **WORLDY** tactics. Remember, your battle is spiritual, and your weapons must be **SPIRITUAL** too!

5) The enemy uses **SPECULATIONS** to attack us by planting '**WHAT IF**' scenarios — negative, demonically inspired thoughts that lead to fear and doubt.

6) **LOFTY THINGS** are those things we perceive as **GREATER** than God's power to solve, designed to make us doubt God's ability or desire to heal.

7) If you go down to the Valley of Ono, you will quickly find yourself saying **OH NO**!

8) When tempted to go down, remind yourself: 'I am doing a **GREAT WORK** for my family, and I cannot afford to stop now!'

9) When standing against the attacks of the enemy, you often don't need '**NEW**' actions, but '**RENEWED**' actions.

10) Never forget, that you can know the enemy's **TACTICS** coming against your restoration, and you possess divine power to **CRUSH** them!

Session 7 - Standing With The Divine Perspective

1) The most important aspect of standing for your marriage restoration is to stand with a **DIVINE PERSPECTIVE**.

2) A major element of standing with a Divine Perspective is **CHOOSING** what you **FOCUS** on.

3) What we focus on is what we **FEEL** and what we feel drives our **ACTIONS.**

4) The Divine Perspective focuses on **GOD'S** faithfulness, not your **SPOUSE'S** attitude or actions.

5) The Divine Perspective knows the power of being **STILL** while standing **FIRM**.

6) The sitting season is an invitation to surrender **CONTROL** and allow God to reveal His power and glory.

7) Be Supernaturally **STUBBORN** regarding the promises of God.

8) The Divine Perspective sets its mind to God's **ABILITY** to **PURSUE** and **TOUCH** our spouse!

9) Know that God is **PURSUING** your spouse even if they are not pursuing Him.

10) God's holy **FIRE** is actively at work in your spouse's life, purifying them from their sins, doubts, and struggles they are facing.

11) The Divine Perspective sets its mind to the truth that God is releasing the **SUPERNATURAL** to fight for your marriage!

12) Pray that the **DIVORCE-BUSTING** angel will deliver that same message to your spouse, reassuring them that they need not fear returning to the marriage.

Session 8 - Standing In Victory

1) There is a **PROPHETIC** promise that God is turning the hearts of family members back to each other!

2) Your spouse's **HEART** is turning back to you!

3) One of the biggest lies the devil tells standers is that you **DON'T** have what it takes and you're not going to **MAKE** it!

4) You **ALREADY** have all the resources needed to stand for your marriage!

5) There is a guaranteed blessing just for **BELIEVING** in the Lord's promises.

6) Stand on the truth that this is the season of your life when you are going to **PROSPER** in all things!

7) Love is the greatest **MOTIVATOR** on Earth.

8) Love creates **PERSEVERANCE** like nothing else can.

9) Love removes **FEAR**.

10) Love brings **QUIETNESS** and peace.

11) Love **NEVER** fails!

12) It is standing in **CHRIST'S LOVE**, not your love, that will bring you victory!

Session 9 - A Spouse's Perspective

1) You have the power to carry **HOPE** for your marriage, even if your spouse has lost hope.

2) The enemy is the greatest **DECEIVER** ever! He presents himself in a way that appears good and harmless, making it easy for your spouse to fall into his traps.

3) You have the power to **PRAY** and have your spouse's eyes **OPENED** so they can see!

4) Don't be shocked if you hear your spouse **SAY** somebody said it's ok to leave, or that it's **OK** they are moving on.

5) God **HAS NOT** given up on your spouse; He is still pursuing them even if your spouse may not be **PURSUING** God.

6) God's love and kindness, not **CONDEMNATION**, is what brings change and healing to your spouse.

7) Your faith can **SEE** what your spouse's eyes cannot.

8) Never lose hope that God can change hearts **SUDDENLY** and unexpectedly. What seems impossible one day can become a **REALITY** the very next day!

9) If we are **FORGIVEN** much, the Bible says that we **LOVE** much.

10) Never forget, God is able to do far **MORE** than you can even dream and **IMAGINE**.

APPENDIX: SCRIPTURE LIST

Scripture List

Session 1 – Foundations of Standing Supernaturally

Luke 1:37 (ESV) *"For nothing will be impossible with God."*

Job 9:10 (NIV) *"He performs wonders that cannot be fathomed, miracles that cannot be counted."*

Matthew 19:5–6 (ESV) *"and said, 'Therefore a man shall leave his father and his mother and hold fast to his wife, and the two shall become one flesh'? ⁶So they are no longer two but one flesh. What therefore God has joined together, let not man separate."*

Hebrews 11:1 (NIV) *"Now faith is confidence in what we hope for and assurance about what we do not see."*

Joel 2:25–26 (ESV) ²⁵*"I will restore to you the years that the swarming locust has eaten, the hopper, the destroyer, and the cutter, my great army, which I sent among you.* ²⁶*"You shall eat in plenty and be satisfied, and praise the name of the Lord your God, who has dealt wondrously with you. And my people shall never again be put to shame."*

Lamentations 5:21 (NIV) *"Restore us to yourself, Lord, that we may return; renew our days as of old."*

Jeremiah 30:17 (NIV) *"But I will restore you to health and heal your wounds,' declares the Lord, 'because you are called an outcast, Zion for whom no one cares.'"*

1 Peter 5:10 (NIV) *"And the God of all grace, who called you to his eternal glory in Christ, after you have suffered a little while, will himself restore you and make you strong, firm and steadfast."*

Zechariah 9:12 (NIV) *"Return to your fortress, you prisoners of hope; even now I announce that I will restore twice as much to you."*

Ezekiel 36:26 (NIV) *"I will give you a new heart and put a new spirit in you; I will remove from you your heart of stone and give you a heart of flesh."*

Psalm 147:3 (NIV) *"He heals the brokenhearted and binds up their wounds."*

Jeremiah 32:27 (NIV) *"I am the LORD, the God of all mankind. Is anything too hard for me?"*

Romans 15:13 (NIV) *"May the God of hope fill you with all joy and peace as you trust in him, so that you may overflow with hope by the power of the Holy Spirit."*

Session 2: Spiritual Warfare Over Marriages

John 10:10 (NIV) *"The thief comes only to steal and kill and destroy; I have come that they may have life, and have it to the full."*

Ephesians 5:31-32 (NIV) *"For this reason a man will leave his father and mother and be united to his wife, and the two will become one flesh. This is a profound mystery—but I am talking about Christ and the church."*

1 Peter 5:8 (NIV) *"Be alert and of sober mind. Your enemy the devil prowls around like a roaring lion looking for someone to devour."*

Ephesians 6:12 (NIV) *"For our struggle is not against flesh and blood, but against the rulers, against the authorities, against the powers of this dark world and against the spiritual forces of evil in the heavenly realms."*

2 Corinthians 2:11 (NLT) *"so that Satan will not outsmart us. For we are familiar with his evil schemes."*

2 Corinthians 2:11 (MSG) *"After all, we don't want to unwittingly give Satan an opening for yet more mischief—we're not oblivious to his sly ways!*

2 Corinthians 4:4 (NIV) *"The god of this age has blinded the minds of unbelievers, so that they cannot see the light of the gospel of the glory of Christ, who is the image of God."*

2 Corinthians 4:4 (TPT) *"for their minds have been blinded by the god of this age, leaving them in unbelief. Their blindness keeps them from seeing the dayspring light of the wonderful news of the glory of Jesus Christ, who is the divine image of God."*

1 John 3:8 (NIV) *"The reason the Son of God appeared was to destroy the devil's work."*

Luke 10:19 (NIV) *"I have given you authority to trample on snakes and scorpions and to overcome all the power of the enemy; nothing will harm you."*

Romans 16:20 (NIV) *"The God of peace will soon crush Satan under your feet. The grace of our Lord Jesus be with you."*

Session 3: Reconciliation and Repentance

2 Corinthians 5:17–20 (NIV) "¹⁷Therefore, if anyone is in Christ, he is a new creation; the old has gone, the new has come! ¹⁸All this is from God, who reconciled us to himself through Christ and gave us the ministry of reconciliation: ¹⁹that God was reconciling the world to himself in Christ, not counting men's sins against them. And he has committed to us the message of reconciliation. ²⁰We are therefore Christ's ambassadors, as though God were making his appeal through us. We implore you on Christ's behalf: Be reconciled to God."

Psalm 139:23–24 (NIV) "²³Search me, O God, and know my heart; test me and know my anxious thoughts. ²⁴See if there is any offensive way in me, and lead me in the way everlasting."

Acts 3:19 (NIV) "Repent, then, and turn to God, so that your sins may be wiped out, that times of refreshing may come from the Lord."

Luke 15:16–24 (NIV) "¹⁶He longed to fill his stomach with the pods that the pigs were eating, but no one gave him anything. ¹⁷"When he came to his senses, he said, 'How many of my father's hired men have food to spare, and here I am starving to death! ¹⁸I will set out and go back to my father and say to him: Father, I have sinned against heaven and against you. ¹⁹I am no longer worthy to be called your son; make me like one of your hired men.' ²⁰So he got up and went to his father. "But while he was still a long way off, his father saw him and was filled with compassion for him; he ran to his son, threw his arms around him and kissed him. ²¹"The son said to him, 'Father, I have sinned against heaven and against you. I am no longer worthy to be called your son.' ²²"But the father said to his servants, 'Quick! Bring the best robe and put it on him. Put a ring on his finger and sandals on his feet. ²³Bring the fattened calf and kill it. Let's have a feast and celebrate. ²⁴For this son of mine was dead and is alive again; he was lost and is found.' So they began to celebrate."

Hebrews 12:5-7 (NIV) "And have you completely forgotten this word of encouragement that addresses you as a father addresses his son? It says, 'My son, do not make light of the Lord's discipline, and do not lose heart when he rebukes you, because the Lord disciplines the one he loves, and he chastens everyone he accepts as his son.' Endure hardship as discipline; God is treating you as his children. For what children are not disciplined by their father?"

Galatians 6:1 (NIV) "Brothers and sisters, if someone is caught in a sin, you who live by the Spirit should restore that person gently. But watch yourselves, or you also may be tempted."

Romans 2:4b (NIV) "... not realizing that God's kindness leads you toward repentance?"

Acts 5:31 (NIV) "God exalted him to his own right hand as Prince and Savior that he might give repentance and forgiveness of sins to Israel."

Acts 11:18 (ESV) "When they heard these things they fell silent. And they glorified God, saying, "Then to the Gentiles also God has granted repentance that leads to life."

2 Timothy 2:24–26 (ESV) "²⁴And the Lord's servant must not be quarrelsome but kind to everyone, able to teach, patiently enduring evil, ²⁵correcting his opponents with gentleness. God may perhaps grant them repentance leading to a knowledge of the truth, ²⁶and they may come to their senses and escape from the snare of the devil, after being captured by him to do his will.

Romans 4:17–22 (ESV) "¹⁷as it is written, "I have made you the father of many nations"—in the presence of the God in whom he believed, who gives life to the dead and calls into existence the things that do not exist. ¹⁸In hope he believed against hope, that he should become the father of many nations, as he had been told, "So shall your offspring be." ¹⁹He did not weaken in faith when he considered his own body, which was as good as dead (since he was about a hundred years old), or when he considered the barrenness of Sarah's womb. ²⁰No unbelief made him waver concerning the promise of God, but he grew strong in his faith as he gave glory to God, ²¹fully convinced that God was able to do what he had promised. ²²That is why his faith was "counted to him as righteousness."

Session 4: Standing with a Healed Heart: Grief, Shame, Fear and Forgiveness

John 11:35 (ESV) *"Jesus wept."*

Psalm 62:8 (ESV) *"Trust in him at all times, O people; pour out your heart before him; God is a refuge for us."*

1 Peter 5:7 (NIV) *"Cast all your anxiety on him because he cares for you."*

Psalm 34:19 (ESV) *"Many are the afflictions of the righteous, but the LORD delivers him out of them all."*

Matthew 5:4 (NIV) *"Blessed are those who mourn, for they shall be comforted."*

Psalm 25:3a (NIV) *"No one who hopes in you will ever be put to shame..."*

Romans 8:1 (ESV) *"There is therefore now no condemnation for those who are in Christ Jesus."*

Psalm 56:3–4 (NIV) *³"When I am afraid, I will trust in you. ⁴In God, whose word I praise, in God I trust; I will not be afraid. What can mortal man do to me?"*

2 Timothy 1:7 (NKJV) *"For God has not given us a spirit of fear, but of power and of love and of a sound mind."*

1 John 4:18 (NIV) *"There is no fear in love. But perfect love drives out fear, because fear has to do with punishment. The one who fears is not made perfect in love."*

Isaiah 41:10 (NIV) *"So do not fear, for I am with you; do not be dismayed, for I am your God. I will strengthen you and help you; I will uphold you with my righteous right hand."*

Matthew 18:21–23 (NIV) *"²¹Then Peter came to Jesus and asked, "Lord, how many times shall I forgive my brother when he sins against me? Up to seven times?" ²²Jesus answered, "I tell you, not seven times, but seventy-seven times. ²³"Therefore, the kingdom of heaven is like a king who wanted to settle accounts with his servants."*

Colossians 3:13 (NIV) "Bear with each other and forgive one another if any of you has a grievance against someone. Forgive as the Lord forgave you."

2 Corinthians 5:18–19 (NIV) "¹⁸All this is from God, who reconciled us to himself through Christ and gave us the ministry of reconciliation: ¹⁹that God was reconciling the world to himself in Christ, not counting men's sins against them. And he has committed to us the message of reconciliation."

Session 5: The Promise, Price, and Power of Hope

Hebrews 11:1 (ESV) "Now faith is the assurance of things hoped for, the conviction of things not seen."

Matthew 17:20 (NIV) "He replied, "Because you have so little faith. I tell you the truth, if you have faith as small as a mustard seed, you can say to this mountain, 'Move from here to there' and it will move. Nothing will be impossible for you."

Romans 12:6 (NKJV) "Having then gifts differing according to the grace that is given to us, let us use them: if prophecy, let us prophesy in proportion to our faith;"

Hebrews 11:1 (AMP) "NOW FAITH is the assurance (the confirmation, the title deed) of the things [we] hope for, being the proof of things [we] do not see and the conviction of their reality [faith perceiving as real fact what is not revealed to the senses]."

Romans 12:12 (NIV) "Be joyful in hope, patient in affliction, faithful in prayer."

Psalm 51:12 (ESV) "Restore to me the joy of your salvation, and uphold me with a willing spirit."

Nehemiah 8:10b (ESV) "… And do not be grieved, for the joy of the LORD is your strength."

Lamentations 3:25-26 "The LORD is good to those whose hope is in him, to the one who seeks him; it is good to wait quietly for the salvation of the LORD. "

Psalm 25:3 (NIV) "No one who hopes in you will ever be put to shame…"

Romans 15:13 (NIV) "May the God of hope fill you with all joy and peace as you trust in him, so that you may overflow with hope by the power of the Holy Spirit."

Romans 8:24–25 (NIV) "²⁴For in this hope we were saved. But hope that is seen is no hope at all. Who hopes for what he already has? ²⁵But if we hope for what we do not yet have, we wait for it patiently."

Romans 5:3-5 (NIV) "Not only so, but we also glory in our sufferings, because we know that suffering produces perseverance; perseverance, character; and character, hope. And hope does not put us to shame, because God's love has been poured out into our hearts through the Holy Spirit, who has been given to us."

James 1:2-4, 12 (NLT) "2 Dear brothers and sisters, when troubles come your way, consider it an opportunity for great joy. 3 For you know that when your faith is tested, your endurance has a chance to grow. 4 So let it grow, for when your endurance is fully developed, you will be perfect and complete, needing nothing 12 God blesses those who patiently endure testing and temptation. Afterward they will receive the crown of life that God has promised to those who love him."

Colossians 1:11 (NKJV) "strengthened with all might, according to His glorious power, for all patience and longsuffering with joy;"

Galatians 6:9 (NIV) "Let us not become weary in doing good, for at the proper time we will reap a harvest if we do not give up."

Psalm 71:14 "As for me, I will always have hope; I will praise you more and more."

Haggai 2:9 (KJV) "The glory of this latter house shall be greater than of the former, saith the Lord of hosts: And in this place will I give peace, saith the Lord of hosts."

Session 6: Standing Aware of the Enemy's Plans

2 Corinthians 2:11 (NLT) "so that Satan will not outsmart us. For we are familiar with his evil schemes."

2 Corinthians 2:11 (MSG) "After all, we don't want to unwittingly give Satan an opening for yet more mischief—we're not oblivious to his sly ways!"

Galatians 6:9 (NIV) "Let us not become weary in doing good, for at the proper time we will reap a harvest if we do not give up."

2 Corinthians 10:4 (NASB) "for the weapons of our warfare are not of the flesh....., but divinely powerful for the destruction of fortresses."

2 Corinthians 10:5 (NASB) "We are destroying speculations and every lofty thing raised up against the knowledge of God, and we are taking every thought captive to the obedience of Christ,"

Nehemiah 6:1–2 (NKJV) "¹Now it happened when Sanballat, Tobiah, Geshem the Arab, and the rest of our enemies heard that I had rebuilt the wall, and that there were no breaks left in it (though at that time I had not hung the doors in the gates), ²that Sanballat and Geshem sent to me, saying, "Come, let us meet together among the villages in the plain of Ono." But they thought to do me harm."

Nehemiah 6:3 (NKJV) "So I sent messengers to them, saying, "I am doing a great work, so that I cannot come down. Why should the work cease while I leave it and go down to you?"

Nehemiah 6:4 (NKJV) "But they sent me this message four times, and I answered them in the same manner."

Session 7: Standing with The Divine Perspective

Colossians 3:2 (NIV) "Set your minds on things above, not on earthly things."

Romans 12:2 (NIV) "Do not conform any longer to the pattern of this world, but be transformed by the renewing of your mind. Then you will be able to test and approve what God's will is--his good, pleasing and perfect will."

Psalm 2:4 (ESV) "He who sits in the heavens laughs; the Lord holds them in derision."

Luke 1:37 (ESV) "For nothing will be impossible with God."

Job 9:10 (NIV) "He performs wonders that cannot be fathomed, miracles that cannot be counted."

Jeremiah 32:27 (NIV) "I am the LORD, the God of all mankind. Is anything too hard for me?"

Isaiah 43:19 (NLT) "For I am about to do something new. See, I have already begun! Do you not see it? I will make a pathway through the wilderness. I will create rivers in the dry wasteland."

Zechariah 4:6 (ESV) "Then he said to me, "This is the word of the Lord to Zerubbabel: Not by might, nor by power, but by my Spirit, says the Lord of hosts."

John 11:40 (NKJV) "Did I not say to you that if you would believe you would see the glory of God?"

Exodus 14:13–14 (NIV) "[13]Moses answered the people, "Do not be afraid. Stand firm and you will see the deliverance the Lord will bring you today. The Egyptians you see today you will never see again. [14]The Lord will fight for you; you need only to be still.""

Psalm 46:10 (NIV) "Be still, and know that I am God; I will be exalted among the nations, I will be exalted in the earth."

Isaiah 30:15 (NIV) "This is what the Sovereign Lord, the Holy One of Israel, says: "In repentance and <u>rest</u> is your salvation, in <u>quietness</u> and trust is your strength, but you would have none of it.""

2 Chronicles 20:17 (NIV) "You will not have to fight this battle. Take up your positions; stand firm and see the deliverance the Lord will give you, O Judah and Jerusalem. Do not be afraid; do not be discouraged. Go out to face them tomorrow, and the Lord will be with you.'"

Ephesians 6:13 (AMP) "Therefore put on God's complete armor, that you may be able to resist and stand your ground on the evil day [of danger], and, having done all [the crisis demands], to stand [firmly in your place]."

Galatians 6:9 (NIV) "Let us not become weary in doing good, for at the proper time we will reap a harvest if we do not give up."

Isaiah 65:1–2 (NIV) [1]"I revealed myself to those who did not ask for me; I was found by those who did not seek me. To a nation that did not call on my name, I said, 'Here am I, here am I.' [2]All day long I have held out my hands to an obstinate people, who walk in ways not good, pursuing their own imaginations—"

Romans 10:20–21 (NIV) "[20]And Isaiah boldly says, "I was found by those who did not seek me; I revealed myself to those who did not ask for me." [21]But concerning Israel he says, "All day long I have held out my hands to a disobedient and obstinate people.""

Zechariah 2:5 (NASB) "'For I,' declares the Lord, 'will be a wall of fire around her, and I will be the glory in her midst.'"

Malachi 3:3 (NIV) "He will sit as a refiner and purifier of silver; he will purify the Levites and refine them like gold and silver. Then the Lord will have men who will bring offerings in righteousness,"

1 Peter 2:9 (NIV) "But you are a chosen people, a royal priesthood, a holy nation, a people belonging to God, that you may declare the praises of him who called you out of darkness into his wonderful light."

Matthew 1:19–20 (ESV) "[19]And her husband Joseph, being a just man and unwilling to put her to shame, resolved to divorce her quietly. [20]But as he considered these things, behold, an angel of the Lord appeared to him in a dream, saying, "Joseph, son of David, do not fear to take Mary as your wife, for that which is conceived in her is from the Holy Spirit."

Matthew 1:24 (ESV) "When Joseph woke from sleep, he did as the angel of the Lord commanded him: he took his wife,"

Hebrews 1:14 (NIV) "Are not all angels ministering spirits sent to serve those who will inherit salvation?"

Session 8: Standing in Victory

Malachi 4:5–6 (NASB) [5]"Behold, I am going to send you Elijah the prophet before the coming of the great and terrible day of the Lord.[6]"And he will restore the hearts of the fathers to their children, and the hearts of the children to their fathers, lest I come and smite the land with a curse."

Luke 1:15–17 (NASB) [15]"For he will be great in the sight of the Lord, and he will drink no wine or liquor; and he will be filled with the Holy Spirit, while yet in his mother's womb. [16]"And he will turn back many of the sons of Israel to the Lord their God. [17]"And it is he who will go as a forerunner before Him in the spirit and power of Elijah, to turn the hearts of the fathers back to the children, and the disobedient to the attitude of the righteous; so as to make ready a people prepared for the Lord."

Matthew 11:14 (AMP) "And if you are willing to receive and accept it, John himself is Elijah who was to come [before the kingdom]."

2 Corinthians 5:18 (ESV) "All this is from God, who reconciled us to himself through Christ and gave us the ministry of reconciliation."

Ezekiel 11:19 (NIV) "I will give them an undivided heart and put a new spirit in them; I will remove from them their heart of stone and give them a heart of flesh."

Deuteronomy 30:6 (NIV) "The Lord your God will circumcise your hearts and the hearts of your descendants, so that you may love him with all your heart and with all your soul, and live."

Jeremiah 24:7 (NIV) "I will give them a heart to know me, that I am the Lord. They will be my people, and I will be their God, for they will return to me with all their heart."

2 Peter 1:3 (NIV) *"His divine power has given us everything we need for life and godliness through our knowledge of him who called us by his own glory and goodness."*

John 3:34 (ESV) *"For he whom God has sent utters the words of God, for he gives the Spirit without measure."*

Ephesians 1:3 (ESV) *"Blessed be the God and Father of our Lord Jesus Christ, who <u>has</u> blessed us in Christ with every spiritual blessing in the heavenly places,"*

Luke 1:45 (NIV) *"Blessed is she who has believed that what the Lord has said to her will be accomplished!"*

John 11:40 (NKJV) *"Did I not say to you that if you would believe you would see the glory of God?"*

Psalm 84:11 (NIV) *"For the Lord God is a sun and shield; the Lord bestows favor and honor; no good thing does he withhold from those whose walk is blameless."*

Ephesians 1:3 (NIV) *"Praise be to the God and Father of our Lord Jesus Christ, who has blessed us in the heavenly realms with every spiritual blessing in Christ."*

3 John 2 (NKJV) *"Beloved, I pray that you may prosper in all things and be in health, just as your soul prospers"*

Psalm 1:3 (NIV) *"That person is like a tree planted by streams of water, which yields its fruit in season and whose leaf does not wither—whatever they do prospers."*

Jeremiah 29:11 (NIV) *"For I know the plans I have for you, declares the Lord, plans for welfare and not for evil, to give you a future and a hope."*

Psalm 34:10 (NIV) *"The lions may grow weak and hungry, but those who seek the Lord lack no good thing."*

Proverbs 10:22 (NIV) *"The blessing of the Lord brings wealth, without painful toil for it."*

2 Corinthians 5:14a (ESV) *"For the love of Christ controls us,… because we have concluded this: that one has died for all, therefore all have died;"*

2 Corinthians 5:14a (TPT) *"For it is Christ's love that fuels our passion and motivates us, …."*

2 Corinthians 5:14a (MSG) *"Christ's love has moved me to such extremes. His love has the first and last word in everything we do…"*

1 Corinthians 13:4 (ESV) *"Love is patient"*

1 Corinthians 13:7 (ESV) *"Love bears all things, believes all things, hopes all things, endures all things."*

Genesis 29:20 (ESV) *"So Jacob served seven years for Rachel, and they seemed to him but a few days because of the love he had for her."*

1 John 4:18 (ESV) *"There is no fear in love, but perfect love casts out fear. For fear has to do with punishment, and whoever fears has not been perfected in love."*

Zephaniah 3:17 (ESV) *"The LORD your God is in your midst, a mighty one who will save; he will rejoice over you with gladness; he will quiet you by his love; he will exult over you with loud singing."*

1 Corinthians 13:8 (NIV) *"Love never fails. But where there are prophecies, they will cease; where there are tongues, they will be stilled; where there is knowledge, it will pass away."*

Session 9 – A Spouse's Perspective

Psalm 71:14 (NIV) *"As for me, I will always have hope; I will praise you more and more."*

2 Corinthians 11:14 (NASB) *"No wonder, for even Satan disguises himself as an angel of light."*

2 Corinthians 4:4 (NIV) *"The god of this age has blinded the minds of unbelievers, so that they cannot see the light of the gospel that displays the glory of Christ, who is the image of God."*

Isaiah 65:1 (NIV) *"I revealed myself to those who did not ask for me; I was found by those who did not seek me. To a nation that did not call on my name, I said, 'Here am I, here am I.'"*

Romans 2:4 (NASB) *"Or do you think lightly of the riches of His kindness and tolerance and patience, not knowing that the kindness of God leads you to repentance?"*

Hebrews 11:1 (NASB) *"Now faith is the assurance of things hoped for, the conviction of things not seen."*

Proverbs 21:1 (NASB) *"The king's heart is like channels of water in the hand of the Lord; He turns it wherever He pleases."*

Luke 7:47 (NKJV) *"Therefore I say to you, her sins, which are many, are forgiven, for she loved much. But to whom little is forgiven, the same loves little."*

Ephesians 3:20 (NASB) *"Now to Him who is able to do far more abundantly beyond all that we ask or think, according to the power that works within us."*

Made in the USA
Monee, IL
04 July 2025